SAME FAITH SAME GOD

Endorsements

Pastor John W. Stevenson's life of faith all the years I have known him is powerfully laid out in this wonderful book. So many times, in his journey, others have told him that his faith for this or that objective was preposterous—ridiculous! Yet this man would not go away or give up. He is today the man that his God has formed for the journey.

I so admire John. Whenever I hear his voice, I hear the same John I have known and loved as a covenant brother all these years. Consistency is the vindication of his faith. He reflects the same faith that his unchanging God has given him. I applaud his courage to obey what he has heard and proclaim it with confidence. This is a straightforward narrative of John's faith shown through a substantive life.

This book, *Same Faith, Same God: Living in The Realm of Ridiculous Faith*, is an account of his life lived out as a proclamation of his own testimony. I know this work that flowed out of Pastor John's heart will bless everyone who reads it.

Glenn Roachelle, President, Consultant, Gate Ministries

Most people live in perpetual longing for better conditions and circumstances. But Jesus, the eternal Son of God, was born into a bad time and a bad place. Then through His relationship with His Father, He brought the transforming reality of Heaven into His earth space and time. That's what "Heaven on earth" means! And it transformed the whole earth and the course of history. And here's a secret: YOU can live out that same miraculous pattern in your times and places.

That is essentially the message of Pastor Stevenson's wonderful new book. This is a splendid biography, but much more. The story carries the reader into that realm of living, pulsating, dynamic, and ridiculous faith. Through the high drama of the story, the reader begins to understand how to move beyond letting life set the terms of our time on earth or living life on God's terms.

Trust me, *Same Faith, Same God: Living in the Realm of Ridiculous Faith* will knock your shoes off!

Ed Chinn, Author, Editor, Publisher, Cool River Pub

John, thank you for taking the time and energy to write *Same Faith, Same God: Living in the Realm of Ridiculous Faith*. I have so loved our friendship and relationship over the years. Your example of living at this level of faith has not only encouraged me but has shown me a path to live in that same kind of faith. I hope everyone I know will read this book, believe the scriptures and the stories included, so they can also live in the Realm of Ridiculous Faith. It is no surprise that someone who lives a lifestyle of worship and writes the book *Worshiper by Design* would experience this kind of faith and experience the kinds of outcomes that you have experienced. Your lifestyle of worship and lifestyle of faith are an amazing example to many, including me. I highly recommend both of these books to anyone who wants to see God move in amazing ways in their lives. Thank you again, and well done, my friend.

Ford Taylor, Founder FSH Consulting and Transformational Leadership

John W. Stevenson brings the gift of his testimony of the power of God at work in a life of a man who has chosen the one thing that pleases God, faith, and does so by sharing his incredible journey of "ridiculous faith" that will inspire, encourage, and strengthen anyone who cries out to Jesus as the man seeking healing for his son, "Lord, I believe! Help my unbelief!" The author's humility, transparency, and knowledge of the promises of God shine through every page of this book. I have personally sat under the revelation of this message and was deeply inspired and challenged to live a life of ridiculous faith. I encourage you to let this book lead you on a journey to greater faith and trust in God.

Dr. Mike Hutchings, Director, Global Awakening School of Supernatural Ministry

I am thankful that John W. Stevenson has taken us on his journey of growing in faith, ridiculous faith. It is not an easy task to look backwards on more than thirty years to see how God calls and leads a person who desires to hear God for direction of their life. Psalms 107:2 states "Let the redeemed of the Lord tell their story…" By telling his story, he will impact many who are longing to follow God more closely. He has carefully woven many Biblical accounts to illuminate his own story. Read this book and see how you might be led into a faith life that will be considered ridiculous.

Lou Shirey, Director of Thriving Throughout the Seasons of Pastoral Ministry Program, International Pentecostal Holiness Church

Same Faith, Same God is a deeply intimate book. At times, I felt like I had crept into JW's study and was looking over his shoulder as he poured out his story. *Same Faith, Same God* made me divinely uncomfortable. Incredibly rich with personal vulnerability and stories of ridiculous faith, *Same Faith, Same God* is for every believer who desires a more honest, faith-fueled relationship with Jesus. JW takes us on a practical, and at times, painful journey into the depths of his challenges with prostate cancer, ministry, and life itself. *Same Faith, Same God* will challenge you to abandon a superficial understanding of unbelief, contradiction, brokenness, and fear, and discover the joy of wholeness only found at the feet of Jesus. I highly recommend this book for anyone seeking a deeper, more personal understanding of living out a ridiculous faith in Jesus.

Jimmy Dodd, Founder and CEO—PastorServe

We have had the privilege of knowing Apostle John W. Stevenson for over 20 years. John is a worshiper, songwriter, author, and apostolic leader whose influence has and continues to touch nations. In his current written work, *Same Faith, Same God: Living in the Realm of Ridiculous Faith,* he invites us into his world as he navigates through his personal faith journey. You will be enlightened, challenged, and brought face to face with an invitation to enter this realm of Ridiculous Faith. The just shall live by faith.

Bishop Harold & Pastor Fellicia Duncan, The Life Ministries, Detroit, Michigan

Having known Pastor John W. Stevenson for just a few short years, I particularly value the theme of his book, "Living in the Realm of Ridiculous Faith." Pastor John has consistently lived out his faith, as demonstrated in his current mission for The Embassy, to be used to bring change to the City of Hamilton.

Dan Tarkington, Four Seasons Environmental, Inc., Monroe, OH

I have known Apostle John W. Stevenson for over thirty years. I only know a few men of God that have a strong passion to pursue the will of God for their lives as John does. He has exemplified the strong level of faith that the men and women of the Bible displayed. Like those we read about, John has walked through seasons of testings that did not make sense in the natural. No matter what the cost, he yet followed God and paid the price as one of God's elect. I can truly say when I didn't understand, I've witnessed him walk in Ridiculous Faith and he continues to walk in it. John, you inspire me.
Apostle Juan Woods Triumphant Christian Center

Apostle John W. Stevenson is a general in the faith who I am honored to call my spiritual father, pastor, and friend. In his book, *Same Faith, Same God: Living the Realm of Ridiculous Faith*, you will not only read about the principles of faith, but you will also get an inside look how Apostle John lives those principles in his life. You will feel his heart as he shares details of each God-given invitation to live in the Realm of Ridiculous Faith and his acceptance of those invitations. You will also find encouragement to stand firm in your faith while facing seasons of contradiction.

As I read, I could see my own faith journey through Apostle John's journey; I felt this book was written to and for me. I know you will feel the same. I encourage you to be open to how Holy Spirit will speak to you through the events of Apostle John's journey and the revelation of faith within these pages as you accept God's invitation to to live in the *Realm of Ridiculous Faith*.
Jamal Maxsam, Executive Pastor, Heirs Covenant Churh

Often Apostle John W. Stevenson (or, as I endearingly refer to him) has said he is wired differently. I have only recently understood what he meant as I read this book. As challenging and even frustrating as it has been for me, it has helped me grow in my faith and I am sure it will help others. While I am thankful to God for His favor and provision in my life, reading *Same Faith, Same God* has caused me to reflect on my faith journey and ask the same questions AJ has asked.

This book is an inspiring and faith-building story of what happens when you walk in the true definition of ridiculous faith: walking in

sensitivity to Holy Spirit. This same sensitivity has allowed Apostle John to walk in the humility of God while staying steadfast in what God has called him to do. I can testify that God has continually provided what AJ has needed at His perfect time. My wife and I will forever admire and seek teaching from his unshakeable ability to stand firm and wait on God in the midst of the storms and trials.
Jorge Sossa, Outreach Pastor/CFO, Heirs Covenant Church

I have known Apostle John W. Stevenson for about seven years, and it has been a privilege and honor to be a part of his journey. What he has written in his book will help readers walk in ridiculous faith. I have seen him walk in a consistent and profound relationship with God that allows him to move forward by trusting His word with obedience, grace, patience, and faithful expectation. I am excited for others to witness how Apostle John's own experience with his family and in ministry can help them on their own Kingdom journey.
Sandra Sossa, Outreach Pastor, Heirs Covenant Church

This book is a true account of a life lived out loud and faith demonstrated right before my eyes. I have co-labored in ministry with Apostle John W. Stevenson and have been an eyewitness to many of the frontline accounts shared in this book. I can truly say it has encouraged me to believe one more time and has helped keep me steady! I believe it will do the same for all who read it.
Nina M Neal, Pastor, Heirs Covenant Church

SAME
FAITH
SAME
GOD

Living in the Realm of
Ridiculous **Faith**

John W. Stevenson

HEIRS
Media Group
West Chester, OH

Copyright © 2022 by John W. Stevenson
Same Faith, Same God
Living in the Realm of Ridiculous Faith

All rights reserved. No part of this book may be reproduced in any form, including written, electronic, recording, or photocopying, without written permission of the author. The exception would be in the case of brief quotations embodied in the critical articles or reviews and pages where permission is specifically granted by the author.

Although every precaution has been taken to verify the accuracy of the information contained herein, the author and publisher assume no responsibility for errors or omissions. No liability is assumed for damages that may result from the use of information contained within.

Unless otherwise indicated, Bible quotations are taken from The Holy Bible, New American Standard Bible Copyright © 1960, 1962, 1963, 1968, 1971,1972, 1973, 1975, 1977, 1995 by The Lockman Foundation. Used by permission. All rights reserved.

Scriptures indicated NKJV, KJV, MSG, TPT are from:
  The Holy Bible, New King James Version of the Bible. Copyright © 1982 by Thomas Nelson, Inc.
  The Message. Copyright © 1993, 1994, 1995, 1996, 2000 2001, 2002. Used by permission of NavPress Publishing Group
  The Passion Translation®. Copyright © 2017 by BroadStreet Publishing® Group, LLC. Used by permission. All rights reserved. thePassionTranslation.com

Published by Heirs Media Group, West Chester, Ohio
www.jwstevenson.com

Editor and Interior Design: Deborah A. Gaston www.deborahgaston.com
Cover Design: Alicia Redmond www.AliciaRemondministries.com
Photographer: Jairon Roinson, www.litrevision.com
Hair Stylist: Harold Smith www.salon-concepts.com/p/harold-smith

ISBN: 978-0-9745331-4-8
ISBN E-Book: 978-0-9745331-0-0

*This book is dedicated to my wife Marissa,
my children John (Juaacklyn), Leslie, Nicholas (Latoyia),
David (Una) and Christopher and to all my grandchildren.
You are my greatest joy.
It is my prayer that my journey of faith will encourage and
inspire you to explore the unlimited realms of ridiculous faith for
yourselves.*

Contents

Acknowledgments		xv
A Word from the Author		xvii
Foreword by Howard Rachinski		xxi
Foreword by Bishop Joseph L. Garlington		xxiii
Introduction		xxvii
1	By Invitation Only	1
2	The Journey Begins	9
3	Did I Really Hear from God?	15
4	Obedience at All Cost	21
5	Ridiculous Faith: Some Movement Required	27
6	The Next Realm of Possibilities	35
7	Transitions, Transitions, Transitions	41
8	Grace in the Realm of Ridiculous Faith	49
9	Confidently, Consistently, Courageously	55
10	What Are You Requiring of Me?	63
11	The Process of Perfect Timing	73
12	Trust the God of the Process	83
13	Are You Waiting, or Have You Quit?	89
14	A Season of Contradiction	97
15	Passing the Test	107
16	Stepping into the Promised Land	113

About the Author

Acknowledgments

I want to thank all who have been a part of this journey. First and foremost, my family for loving me and living this journey with me.

To all those mentioned in this book, as well as those who may not be mentioned, who have contributed to my life and journey of faith in unique ways. Thank you!

I thank my spiritual father and pastor, Bishop Joseph L. Garlington and Pastor Barbara Garlington for their love and encouragement through the years.

I must thank my HEIRS Covenant Church family for their love and support, and for giving me the opportunity and the privilege of serving as their pastor.

Thank you to my dear friend, Deborah A. Gaston, my writer and editor, for her willingness to take on this project, for the hours of transcribing, writing, rewriting, editing, and pushing me to give more of myself in this book than I have in previous books.

Most of all, I thank God for His love, mercy, and grace. I thank God for saving me and calling me. I thank Him for His faithfulness to me, His Word and for His favor that has been on my life all my life.

A Word from the Author

Years ago, I watched the movie *Vantage Point*. The plot centers around a shooting and explosion that happened in Spain during international treaty talks. The audience gets to see the events through the eyes of three witnesses. Though all three witnessed the same event, they each interpret and report that event differently, depending on where they were positioned at the time as well as their past and recent experiences.

You and I do the same. We all may see and experience the same events from different vantage points, through different lenses, and with different impact.

My desire in writing *Same Faith, Same God* is to inspire and encourage those who read it by sharing my story and journey into the realm of ridiculous faith. I recognize, however, that it is not just *my* journey. It is my family's journey as well. My wife Marissa and our five children—John, Leslie, Nicholas, David, and Christopher—are all a part of the story, all a part this journey. All our children were born within the first seven years of our marriage. It is important that I help you, the reader, recognize that my wife and children were impacted, both positively and negatively, by every choice I made—choices they were often not in agreement with.

In 1997, when Heirs Family Worship Center started, my wife and children were the founding members. As the ministry grew, each took on roles within the church—ushers and greeters, children's ministry, youth ministry, facilities, adult ministry/counseling, worship team, accounting, and board of directors to name a few. While this allowed our family to spend time together, I recognize the line between family and ministry was often blurred. I did not always set boundaries that would consistently demonstrate my family as my priority. My legacy is my children.

In more recent years, my wife and our children, who are now adults, have each shared with me from their "vantage point" how they viewed and were affected by my journey—our journey—of faith. I hadn't completely, understood how each of my children internalized their life as a "pastor's child," desiring, as all children do, more of their father's attention. I hadn't completely recognized nor understood the pressure my wife felt to respond favorably to the call of ministry on my life or the loneliness she felt for many years from my time given to the ministry of others.

Some of the things they shared were painful for me to hear. But I am grateful that it opened the door for much-needed conversations that allowed me to bring clarity to some decisions I made, ask forgiveness where appropriate, and by God's grace, bring healing, where needed, in our relationships. And as I have learned what it means to my wife and each child to support them and be present to them, I have attempted to provide what they need to be confident they are, and have always been, my priority.

Yes, this book is about faith, but it is equally about mercy, grace, repentance, forgiveness, reconciliation, restoration, and love. I present it to you, not as a man of great faith and power, but as a man who is broken before God. As a man who, from the very moment God saved me, has been in passionate pursuit of Him and all He has for me. As a man who has learned—sometimes the hard way—to rely and lean on God. As a man after His glory!

While the Scriptures speak of the great exploits of men and women of faith, we don't always hear about their families and the impact of those exploits on them. There is no descriptive account of Sarah's reaction to Abram saying, "Hey, we are moving. I don't know where, but I'll know when we get there!" There's no account of how the disciples' families responded to them leaving all they had to follow Jesus! And yet, I can only believe that it wasn't as easy as it seems when we read. And when we do read about their response, it wasn't always positive.

There is great reward that comes from choosing to live in the realm of ridiculous faith. Great fulfillment and joy come from choosing to follow Holy Spirit wherever He leads. But it does not come without cost. There is price we pay as we learn to trust God in and for all things. Very often, it is the price of being misunderstood. We rarely see the magnitude of the reward as we're walking through the process; the process can be challenging. It's often only in retrospect that we understand the blessings we now enjoy are a direct result of the choices we made in the past to pursue God no matter what! In the process, we must trust that God will make all things clear and right in His time. And as He does, we see it was worth every sacrifice we made.

I believe the words of a song I wrote many years ago sum up my journey and, in some ways, this book. Every choice, every step has been because He sent me after glory.

It's not the way I would have chosen for me.
It's not the place I would have gone on my own.
But I remember the day I surrendered,
And remember the words He spoke to me—
He sent me after glory!

It's not the plan that I believed would succeed.
It's not the goal that I was once striving for.
But I remember the day I surrendered,
And I remember the words He spoke to me—
He sent me after glory...

He sent me down a road less traveled on.
He told me to be faithful,
And that His grace would keep me strong.
He sent me after glory to a place that few would understand.
He said one day all would clearly see
He sent me after glory.

So let my life, O Lord, bring glory back to You!
I want to live a life that gives you praise.
My one desire, O Lord, is to one day hear You say,
"Well done! Well done!"

You know the plans, plans You have chosen for me,
Plans for my good, more than I could ever see.
So I rejoice in the day I surrendered,
Yes, I rejoice in the words You spoke to me—
You sent me after glory.

And the same God who sent me after glory is sending you!
~John W. Stevenson

FOREWORD

The word "Faith" can incite many emotions—it can be mystifying, cryptic, intriguing, confusing, exciting, and frustrating—all at the same time! To be sure, "Faith" is not defined, nor confined, by the governance of our rationale. However, "Faith" can often be misaligned in one's life due to past experiences, hurts, and misunderstandings. No one is immune from the toxin of misalignment. We all are besieged with painful questions that invade our pursuit of God: How do I believe? How do I grow in faith? How do I activate faith in my circumstance? As the author states, "There will be many times in this process when your day-to-day reality seems inconsistent with the promises of God."

It has been my privilege to have known John W. Stevenson for the past two decades. I have seen him successfully navigate through his personal experiences, hurts, and misunderstandings because of his God-insight on Faith—especially Ridiculous Faith! And my dear friend has so wonderfully captured and conveyed his faith-insights in this book—*Same Faith, Same God.*

Hearing from God is our life nutrition. How to hear from God is our life necessity. Thankfully, John has lived this necessity and is "real" as he describes his life-journey of faith. You can feel his life seasons. And through his illustrative journey, the author has been able to provide us with "faith nuggets" that explode from the pages of this book. You can learn about the difference between change and transition. You can feast on the special insight regarding Ridiculous Faith!

And you will discover answers to this pervading and provoking question: "What do you do when you face a 'what now' moment?"

This book has enabled me to assess my own faith wellness. It has encouraged and enriched my own pursuit of life purpose. It has affirmed the alignment of my faith with God.

Enjoy your faith-alignment and your personal enrichment through this book!

Howard Rachinski, Founder, Christian Copyright Licensing International (CCLI)

FOREWORD

"You won't accomplish the miraculous until you're willing to attempt the ridiculous."
R.H. Williams

"Tell the priests who carry the ark of the covenant: 'When you reach the edge of the Jordan's waters, go and stand in the river.'"
Joshua 3:8 (NIV)

In the late 1990s, I was invited to speak at a large multiracial international conference in Harare, Zimbabwe. My message for the plenary session that day was entitled, "Go Stand in the River." The atmosphere after I spoke was pregnant with faith, and in that moment, Pastor Tom Deuschle approached me with a request to pray for one of the businessmen in his church who was facing a significant challenge in a business venture. Earlier that year, I preached the same message at a conference where the late Morris Chapman, the noted psalmist and songwriter, was also ministering. He wrote a song around the theme of my sermon, and it included this exhortation.

"Go stand in the river, go stand in the river,
Go stand in the river by faith.
You're not going under, but you're going over,
So stand in the river by faith."

I sensed the need to sing those words several times as divine encouragement to continue doing what he had started. I didn't know at the time that those words and his response to them would energize his struggling faith and change the trajectory of his so-called "ridiculous" path from facing the loss of everything to become CEO of the largest telecommunications company in the nation of Zimbabwe.

My wife, Barbara, and I ministered to the man and his wife, knowing only that he was facing some dire challenges in his business. We knew absolutely nothing about him except that he had a critical need to hear from God. The back story was classically David and Goliath. Goliath was the Zimbabwe government led by a corrupt president and political party who steadfastly resisted his vision to start a telecommunications company in the nation. Since they would not control it, they refused to give him lawful permission to do it. His resources were minuscule compared to those of the government and his detractors. However, he was a man of faith and prayer who refused to be distracted from his goal. Shortly after, he won the battle, his persistence and dedication unleashed the miraculous, and his faith became sight. His company is now the largest provider of telecommunications in Zimbabwe, with branches in many other nations.

There are several insights we can gain from the story in Joshua 3. First of all, at the Red Sea, which divided before they crossed, they were told to stand still (on the shore). However, their instructions now were to stand in the river until the waters had subsided. Secondly, the Jordan River was a rapidly flowing body of water since it was at flood stage! In addition to these and other factors, there is the time factor. They had to wait for a prolonged period before they would see the end of the water flowing past them. I believe the Bible is notorious for "hiding" the time factor, or maybe we are unwilling to recognize how much time it may take to see an answer to prayer. An event in the Bible can take less than five minutes to read, while at the same time, it depicts a journey that in reality took weeks, months, and even years to accomplish.

John Stevenson is a spiritual son in whom I am well pleased. He is a multi-gifted vessel to whom the Father has entrusted much. However, as it says in scripture, "To whom much is given, much is required." I have observed his life and ministry through decades of relationship, and I see in him the "same kind of faith…" I often meet leaders who are struggling with disappointment due to their failure to read the whole story in the Book. One of my mentors once told a group of leaders, "The pathway to ruling is protected and guarded by problems that only men and women of Spirit-given wisdom and godly character can solve." The Bible says that God tested Abraham; I believe He will not allow anyone to arrive at their destination without solving the problems that guard the path.

I have often imagined what the onlookers thought when they saw Jesus spit on the ground and form a paste with his thumb and fingers and then apply to the eyes of a man born blind. Ridicule is the last resort of the cynic unwilling to accept an event in the supernatural realm. Faith and risk are synonyms that embody the possibility of either an OMG breakthrough or an epic failure. But Henry Ford said, "Failure is only the opportunity to more intelligently begin again." I believe true wisdom often disguises itself in the cloak of ridiculousness; I would paraphrase Jesus' words to read, "True wisdom may initially appear ridiculous, but will ultimately be vindicated by its miraculous outcome."

This book will encourage you no matter where you are in your faith journey. The author is genuinely the real deal.

Bishop Joseph L. Garlington, Sr
Founding Pastor of Covenant Church of Pittsburgh
Presiding Bishop, Reconciliation! An International Network of Churches and Ministries

Same Faith, Same God

Introduction

For in it the righteousness of God is revealed from faith to faith; as it is written, "The just shall live by faith."
Romans 1:17 NKJV

A New Normal!

The world as we have known it has changed! As I write, a strain of virus, shrouded in so many unknowns, has rocked the world on every level. The media coverage of the pandemic has incited fear and panic in many—believers and nonbelievers alike. Many are making decisions that govern their daily lives rooted in fear rather than in faith coupled with wisdom. This is evident by recent raids on grocery stores, leaving shelves empty as consumers hoard cleaning supplies, water, food, and for some odd reason, toilet paper. The virus has impacted every area of life: businesses have closed, schools have moved to distant learning, and theaters and movie productions have been shut down, restaurants have shifted to carry-out only, if not completely closing their doors. As a result, the economy has taken a big hit. Many, unfortunately, have lost their jobs, causing even more uncertainty and fear.

Even the Church has been impacted. Church leaders have had to create new ways of reaching people amid numerous restrictions, stay-at-home orders, mask mandates, social distancing and other CDC guidelines—don't touch, don't hug, don't sing. While it has been a challenge, this has been a good thing, for it has forced many to think out of the box and embrace technology to reach even more people. But as more and more individuals opt to worship at home, the local Church is left asking how we walk out faith uncompromisingly in a world plagued with fear.

That in which many once placed their security no longer seems secure; that in which many once trusted, now seems untrustworthy;

that which many held as certain is now clouded with doubt and uncertainty in this "new norm."

However, there is a "norm" that God has established in His Word for the believer. It is not new; it is the way God has always purposed for His people to live. It is the norm the prophet Habakkuk spoke of when he wrote:

"...but the just shall live by his faith" (Habakkuk 2:4b).

In times of change and uncertainty, we must remember that the believer's life is a life of faith. Our ability to rise above every circumstance, to not only live victoriously but live in a way that positively impacts our world and advances the Kingdom of God, rests in walking out our faith with intentionality. It lies in our willingness to step courageously into a realm of faith that may seem absurd, unreasonable, or irrational to others, but is one that distinguishes us from those who do not know the Lord. We must choose to remain in that place of faith—no matter what is going on around us—to see God fulfill His Word in and through us. We must remain steadfast in that faith so others see the power of God in our lives and are drawn to Him. In times like these, we must choose to live in the *Realm of Ridiculous Faith* and make that our norm!

We often marvel at those we read about in the Bible, those who did great things for God, those through whom He worked in powerful ways, those who impacted not only their generation, but also the generations that followed. We long to experience His resurrection power as the early Church did, to see the reality of Jesus' words that declared we'd do "greater works." We want to advance His Kingdom and impact our world. We must recognize that all the mighty men and women of Scripture, who God moved through or on behalf of, had the same thing in common: they all stepped into the realm of Ridiculous Faith—the place that allowed them to access the unprecedented manifestation and demonstration of God's power!

There's no way to get around it. To live in the reality of God's Kingdom, to live a life that's pleasing to Him, takes faith. And not just any kind of faith; it takes ridiculous faith! A faith that causes some to shake their heads and wonder if you've lost your mind. If you and I are going to see God's Kingdom manifest on earth and see His glory displayed, if we are to walk out purpose and destiny, we must be willing to step into this realm and live there, knowing that the same God who moved then, is the same God who is moving in our lives today.

Same Faith, Same God: Living in the Realm of Ridiculous Faith is the result of years of learning to trust God, to stand on His Word, to listen for His Voice, and respond in faith to each invitation He has extended to me. All I wanted from the moment I gave Him my life was to please Him. Hebrews 11:6 tells us: **"But without faith it is impossible to please Him, for he who comes to God must believe that He is, and that He is a rewarder of those who diligently seek Him."** And so over and over and over again, God has presented me with opportunities to exercise faith. He'd speak something to me, show me something He desired for me or desired to do through me—something that seemed anything but sane, rational, or even responsible, something that seemed ridiculous. Then He'd invite me to step into the realm of ridiculous faith to see those things become reality. Each time He extended the invitation, I had a choice to make. I could say "yes," exercise my faith and see His faithfulness to perform His Word, or I could play it safe and never experience all God had for me. Each "yes" was an opportunity to strengthen my faith, to trust God more deeply, to be changed, and to allow God to show me things I may never have known by remaining in the place of the reasonable and rational.

I admit it hasn't always been easy. I admit I've not walked it out perfectly. But God has always been gracious and merciful to get me back on course by sending a word of encouragement and, when needed, a word of correction. He'd realign my thinking with His Word, calling me to repent. He has always been faithful to release His grace in greater measure to enable me to stay on course. And He has never ceased to amaze me by doing "exceeding abundantly above" all I could dream or imagine.

The Lord wants to do the same for you. He is inviting you to live in the realm of endless possibilities—the realm where you can live the life that He has designed for you. I often say we don't know what God can do; we only know what He has done. When we choose to accept His invitation, we are positioned to see more of that which He can do and desires to do on our behalf.

I believe that maybe more than any other time in your life, God is calling you to this realm of ridiculous faith. The stage has been set for you to exercise the same faith the great men and women in the Word exercised…

- *The same faith that caused Abraham to leave all that was comfortable and familiar to him and follow God to an unknown land, with the promise that the entire world would be blessed through him.*
- *The same faith that caused Isaac to prosper greatly in a time of famine because of his obedience to a word from God.*
- *The same faith that caused Gideon to lead an army of 300 into battle against the Midianites' tens of thousands and win.*
- *The same faith that caused David to confidently confront and defeat Goliath.*
- *The same faith that caused Esther to risk her life and go, uninvited, before the king to save a nation.*
- *The same faith that prompted Peter to step out of the boat and walk on water.*
- *The same faith that Peter and John exercised to heal a lame man sitting at the Gate Beautiful, and then boldly claim before the Sanhedrin that they must obey God rather than man.*
- *The same faith that enabled the apostles to cast out demons, heal the sick, raise the dead and declare the Kingdom of God.*
- *The same faith that caused the Apostle Paul to advance the Kingdom of God and establish His Church throughout the then-known world.*

When you choose to live by that same faith, you can rest assured the same God who worked miraculously in the lives of these and countless others will move in unparalleled ways in yours. It is the same God who empowers you, anoints you, provides miraculously for you, and desires to work powerfully through you! It is this same God who now calls you to live in the *Realm of Ridiculous Faith*!

It is my prayer that as I share my journey and the lessons and

INTRODUCTION

principles I've learned along the way, Holy Spirit will speak personally to you, shift your perspective, and forever change how you walk out your faith. I pray where you may have stalled in your faith walk, Holy Spirit will give you the nudge you need to step into this realm, and exercise your faith in ways you never have before to see God do what you've never seen Him do before. May you learn to live in this realm and fulfill purpose and destiny as God has always intended. May you experience His love, grace, faithfulness and power in deeper, fuller ways as God positions you to be a conduit of blessing and one who impacts future generations.

God is inviting you today to live in this *Realm of Ridiculous Faith*. Accept His invitation and be amazed!

Chapter One

By Invitation Only

Now faith is the certainty of things hoped for, a proof of things not seen. For by it the people of old gained approval. By faith we understand that the world has been created by the word of God so that what is seen has not been made out of things that are visible.

Hebrews 11:1-3

The atmosphere was electric. The sound of celebration and thanksgiving filled the air, and God's Presence was almost tangible. I stood on the platform in the sanctuary of The Embassy, the new home of Heirs Covenant Church, looking out over the congregation filled with members and friends who'd come to celebrate the faithfulness and goodness of God with us. This was the "hidden treasure" that had been prophesied to me. This was the fulfillment of God's word! Waves of gratitude swept over me as I thought of how God had brought us to this place.

To many, the very thought of possessing this property had seemed absurd. I remember bringing a few of our leaders here months earlier. We sat in the sanctuary, and I asked, "Can you see us here?" Some were able to see past our natural circumstances and believe this was what God had for us; others did not have that same conviction. They felt the property too large in light of the size of our congregation. They thought it too expensive. The distance too far for many to drive. It was too great a risk. Still, others questioned even going through the process; there was no way we'd even be approved for a loan. "Perhaps," some suggested, "we should focus on something we know we can handle right now!"

I had done that before. Had reduced God's promise to something

I could manage—reduced it in such a way that didn't require much, if any, faith. I knew God was drawing me and our entire body out of that place into a greater place of faith. I could sense God asking, *"Will you trust Me?"* God was inviting us to step into a place of faith that I'd taught and preached about for years. This was an opportunity He was setting before me, before our fellowship, to see what He would do if we'd raise our expectation and believe for the seemingly impossible. I couldn't settle for what we could easily manage.

God was inviting us into the realm of ridiculous faith, and I would not decline the invitation.

A Lifetime of Opportunity

This was not the first time God had presented me with such an opportunity. The fact is my life has been filled with opportunities to trust Him for what appeared to be ridiculous. I'm sure if you look back over your life, you will see the numerous times He has called you to operate in a crazy kind of faith as well. You and I are given many opportunities throughout our lifetime not just to exercise faith but to exercise *ridiculous* faith. Every believer receives multiple invitations to stretch his or her faith in a way that looks and feels totally absurd, even irrational, and to trust the God who specializes in the ridiculous.

> *Living in the realm of ridiculous faith is by invitation only. But it is not an invitation that God extends only to a select few. He invites every believer!*

Living in the realm of ridiculous faith is by invitation only. But it is not an invitation that God extends only to a select few. He invites every believer! God may speak to you or give you a glimpse of what He has for you, as He did Abram. Then He simply says, *"Believe in Me! Walk with Me in this new realm!"*

The Bible tells us that God appeared to Abram while he was in Mesopotamia (Acts 7:2,3) and instructed him to leave everything that was familiar to him, with this promise:

And I will make you a great nation,
And I will bless you, and make your name great;
And so you shall be a blessing;

And I will bless those who bless you,
And the one who curses you I will curse.
And in you all the families of the earth will be blessed
(Genesis 12:2-3).

How ridiculous that must have sounded to Abram! To be the father of many nations, when at 75, he'd yet to father one heir! God was inviting Abram to have faith for what appeared to be ridiculous. It had nothing to do with his age, culture, past experience, wealth, or status in the community. God had chosen him to step into a place of faith that would ultimately change the world, and now Abram had to choose. He could have easily said, "Well…I am 75 years old. I've got a pretty good set up here—financially stable, set to inherit the family idol-making business, all my friends and family are here. Pull up stakes and follow You, a God I don't know very well, to some unknown place? I just don't know. This is so ridiculous! Everyone will think I am out of my mind. Maybe you should choose someone else—someone younger with not much to lose if it doesn't work out. I think I'm good right here in Ur."

> *You see, you don't stumble into the realm of ridiculous faith; you don't accidentally land there. You must make a conscious decision once you have received the Father's invitation!*

But Abram chose to accept the invitation. His willingness to trust the word of God to him and simply say, "Okay," moved him into the realm of ridiculous faith. His "yes" positioned him to see God do the unprecedented on his behalf. It also moved him into purpose and destiny—a destiny that impacted all generations to come. It set him on course to be transformed into Abraham. His "yes" began the process that made him "the father of our faith" (Romans 4:12).

And you must make the choice! You see, you don't stumble into the realm of ridiculous faith; you don't accidentally land there. You must make a conscious decision once you have received the Father's invitation! In every generation, God is looking for those who will accept His offer, but you must *choose* to live there.

You're Going the Wrong Way

I remember so vividly when God first invited me into this realm. In 1980, I was newly married and had moved my bride, Marissa, from Columbus, Ohio to Los Angeles, California. I had a plan. I'd become rich and famous (and, of course, give all the glory to God). Sure, I'd do ministry, but I was after fame and fortune. I didn't realize then that something in me needed to die if I was going to walk out God's purposes and plans for my life. He'd taken me to the other side of the country to begin the process.

I worked in a bank in Beverly Hills, biding my time until my big break. I had connected with a gentleman who was also a songwriter, and we began writing songs together. We knew that if we were to be "discovered," we would need to go into the studio and cut a demo. We began to discuss studio options.

"What about Phillip?" his wife asked one afternoon when we were discussing our plans. "He has a studio. Why don't you just call him?"

"Phillip who?" I asked.

"Phillip Bailey."

"Phillip Bailey? Earth, Wind & Fire, Phillip Bailey?" Growing up, I had idolized the band Earth, Wind & Fire. Their musical arrangements were like no one else's! I'd often thought if I had a band, I wanted them to emulate EWF. And now not only did I have an opportunity to meet one of their members, but I could also be working in the studio with him! God had to be the one opening this door of opportunity for me.

My wife and our newborn son had flown back to Ohio to spend time with family for a month. When I met Phillip and realized he was also a believer, I was convinced it was yet another confirmation that God had sanctioned this collaboration. We began making plans, but as he shared what he wanted to do and how he'd need to do it, I was uneasy. It wasn't lining up with what I believed the Lord was speaking to me. But I was so caught up in the association that I was willing to compromise my convictions. I am sure the enemy thought he had me.

> *You can turn around and go the way I have chosen for you, and I will be with you all the days of your life.*

I was heading to work at the bank one morning, thinking of all the doors that were about to open for me in the music industry. I stepped out of my apartment, and Holy Spirit was waiting for me. "*You're going the wrong way*," He said.

"What do you mean?" I asked.

And then He spoke these words, words that forever changed the trajectory of my life. He said, "*You can go the way that you're going, and you'll have fame, and you'll have success, but you won't have My Presence. Or you can turn around and go the way I have chosen for you, and I will be with you all the days of your life.*"

His words shook me to my core.

Where Will You Live?

I was wrecked for the rest of the day, so much so I could barely work. I now recognize this as God's initial invitation to live in and from a different place of faith in Him. He was willing to give me what I desired, but there was a cost. There is always a cost! I imagine this was how Moses felt when God instructed him to leave Sinai and go to the Promised Land with the children of Israel. God would honor His Word to the children of Israel by giving them the land He had promised Abraham, but because of their stubbornness, He would not go into the land with them (Ex. 33:1-3). Moses responded to the Lord with these words: **"...*If Your Presence does not go with us, do not bring us up from here.*"** Moses knew that the promise without the Presence was empty and dangerous. And at that moment, I knew the price of the fame and success I sought was too great if it meant His Presence wasn't with me.

There is a point in all our lives when we must decide. This is something different from the decision to accept Christ as our Savior; this is the decision to make Him the Lord of *every* area of our lives. It is a decision to follow Him no matter what, to lay down our dreams and desires in order to live the dreams and desires He has for us. It's the decision to know Him more intimately and trust Him implicitly. It is the decision to step into a realm of faith that allows us to see Him do more in and through our lives than we could ever imagine.

What Will You Choose?

Our dreams and desires can become idols that we worship and exalt before God. In Deuteronomy 30:15-20, Moses tells the people they must choose. They must make a choice to serve God or serve the idols in the land.

> *"See, I have set before you today life and prosperity, and death and adversity; in that I command you today to love the Lord your God, to walk in His ways and to keep His commandments and His statutes and His judgments, that you may live and multiply, and that the Lord your God may bless you in the land where you are entering to possess it. But if your heart turns away and you will not obey, but are drawn away and worship other gods and serve them, I declare to you today that you shall surely perish. You will not prolong your days in the land where you are crossing the Jordan to enter and possess it. I call heaven and earth to witness against you today, that I have set before you life and death, the blessing and the curse. So choose life in order that you may live, you and your descendants, by loving the Lord your God, by obeying His voice, and by holding fast to Him; for this is your life and the length of your days, that you may live in the land which the Lord swore to your fathers, to Abraham, Isaac, and Jacob, to give them."*

Many years later, Joshua speaks these same words to the generation he has led into the Promised Land. He tells them that they can serve the gods of their fathers, serve the idols in the land they have just entered, or choose to serve the Lord:

> *"Now, therefore, fear the Lord and serve Him in sincerity and truth; and put away the gods which your fathers served beyond the River and in Egypt, and serve the Lord. If it is disagreeable in your sight to serve the Lord, choose for yourselves today whom you will serve: whether the gods which your fathers served which were beyond the River, or the gods of the Amorites in whose land you are living; but as for me and my house, we will serve the Lord"* **(Joshua 24:14,15).**

In both cases, the people were given the opportunity to choose for themselves. And just like Abraham, Moses, and Joshua, you must choose.

God knows you. Long before you were born, He had a purpose and destiny in mind for you. God knows the path He desires for you to take, but He doesn't coerce you or violate your will. He invites you to walk with Him, with promises He alone can fulfill. He wants you to choose Him above all else, and allow Him to place His desires in your heart (Psalm 37:4). He wants you to *choose* to trust Him completely and *choose* to exercise your faith to see Him bring those desires to fruition. He wants you to *choose* to live in the realm of ridiculous faith.

You and I must choose where we will live, and it is a choice we must make daily. To choose the realm of ridiculous faith will mean laying down everything. It is the decision to die to the flesh, to let go of our pride, ego, dreams and desires and embrace all God desires for us. It is a conscious decision to lay down our reputation, comfort, and anything that we may unknowingly place before God. To live in that place—the place that is pleasing to the Father—means allowing Him to do the necessary work in us by surrendering to both His will and His way.

> *The Realm of Ridiculous Faith is the realm of God's Kingdom that accesses the unprecedented manifestation and demonstration of the power of God.*

What opportunity is the Lord making available to you? In what ways does He want you to participate in the incredible things He is doing in the earth? What does He desire to show you that is beyond anything you can do in your own power and strength? I can assure you that He is inviting you to join Him in this realm of ridiculous faith. It may seem ridiculous to you, but it's not ridiculous to Him.

The Realm of Ridiculous Faith is the realm of God's Kingdom—
- *that accesses the unprecedented manifestation and demonstration of the power of God.*
- *where reputation, position, possessions, dignity and authority have all been abandoned for the sake of the fulfillment of God's divine calling and will.*
- *that assaults the logical, challenges the practical, resists*

> *the reasonable, defies the definitive, confounds the comfortable, and staggers the stability of the status quo.*
> - *that is the realm of Infinite Possibilities only limited by one's inability to believe that WITH GOD ALL THINGS ARE POSSIBLE!*

Know that the Father is inviting you to go to a place you've never been before so He can show you things you never seen before. He wants to show you His unlimited, unmatched power to perform the impossible.

Chapter Two

The Journey Begins

Yet he did not waver through unbelief regarding the promise of God, but was strengthened in his faith and gave glory to God, being fully persuaded that God had power to do what he had promised.

Romans 4:20-21 (NIV)

Not long after God spoke to me, my family and I left California. I didn't know exactly what He had for me, but I knew it wasn't in Los Angeles. My willingness to leave LA demonstrated that I believed what God had spoken. I wish I could say the moment I said yes to God's invitation, everything began to line up perfectly for me and my family; that doors of opportunity immediately opened, and it was smooth sailing from that point on. But that is not the reality of life, and it is not the reality of life in the Kingdom. My acceptance of God's invitation was only the first step of the journey and the first step of the process through which I'd develop my faith, learn to trust God in increasing ways, and be transformed.

As you and I journey to this new realm of faith, we are responsible for growing and maturing our faith. The Apostle Paul tells us that *"... **God has allotted to each a measure of faith**"* (Romans 12:3b). I believe that we all begin our life in Christ with the same amount of faith, the measure we must have to receive God's gift of salvation. We enter His Kingdom and receive eternal life by faith (Ephesians 2:8). However, God desires that our faith moves beyond saving faith and we learn to live each day of our lives by faith. Faith must be the dominant force in the believer's life, and the longer we walk with the Lord, the stronger our faith should be. The onus is on us.

God desires that we mature in faith so that we can believe and trust Him for *anything*, and when He presents us with the "ridiculous," we respond in faith and obedience without wavering. We take the "measure of faith" we have been given, and we exercise it. We cooperate with the Word of the Lord by doing what we know to do. That is our responsibility if we are to see God's good intentions for us come to pass and if we are to live a life that is pleasing to Him.

> **Faith must be the dominant force in the believer's life, and the longer we walk with the Lord, the stronger our faith should be. That is our responsibility.**

I want to make this clear: not everything the Lord calls you to do requires ridiculous faith. But you can be sure that if you are going to walk out purpose and destiny, if you are going to complete your Kingdom assignment in any given season of your life, God will place something before you that is so great, so beyond your ability, so beyond the realm of reason that you will need to exercise this kind of faith. Responding to God in faith and obedience each time He speaks fuels you and prepares you to respond with ridiculous faith when the opportunity presents itself.

The Process of Preparation

The process begins by hearing a word from the Lord and stepping out in faith without having all the specifics. We see this in the life of Abraham. God appeared to him, invited him to embark on the journey of a lifetime, and Abram accepted the invitation. Genesis 12:4 tells us that Abram **went forth as the Lord had spoken to him**…His faith was evident in his act of obedience.

We read in Hebrews 11:3, **"By faith Abraham, when he was called, obeyed by going out to a place which he was to receive for an inheritance; and he went out, not knowing where he was going"** (NKJV). Abram didn't have the full plan; he didn't have a road map, and his faith was far from perfect, but he exercised faith in God's word by leaving Ur and trusting God to lead him to the place He'd promised.

I'm sure this was a giant step for Abram. It had to be a bit daunting. After all, he was just coming to know God, and he was leaving all he'd known for 75 years. But he took the first step—the first of many he would take to become the "Father of Many Nations." I don't believe Abram knew he was entering a process that would prepare him for the promise and prepare him for the ultimate test of faith. Neither did he know how long that process would take. But each time God honored His word, Abraham's faith was bolstered, and he continued to move with God. Eventually his faith in God was so strong that he displayed the ultimate demonstration of ridiculous faith—willingness to sacrifice his only son, Isaac.

There were moments in Abraham's life when reality didn't line up with the word of the Lord to him, and I imagine there were as many opportunities for him to return to what he'd known. Yet, despite how things looked, Abram continued moving forward. He didn't abort the process. We know as we read through the account of his life that Abram made some poor choices and wrong moves. He did not perfectly walk out his faith. It is the same for you and me. As you and I endeavor to move deeper into the realm of ridiculous faith, we won't walk it out perfectly. But I believe that God would rather we move, no matter how imperfect our faith may be and no matter how small the steps we take, than not move at all. God isn't concerned about us getting it perfectly right; He wants to perfect us, to mature us, to prepare us and to transform us in the process. When we get off course, He lovingly steers us in the right direction. There is grace to mess up, grace to get up, and grace to keep moving forward.

> *When we get off course, He lovingly steers us in the right direction. There is grace to mess up, grace to get up, and grace to start moving forward.*

Life on Whose Terms?

I moved my family back to Columbus, Ohio so I could get a sense of what God wanted to do in my life. Marissa and I returned to the church where we'd met, and I got a job to support our growing family. During that season of my life, I worked several jobs, from screen printing to working for Children's Services in a group home and as a rep for a labor union, but I had no real sense of satisfaction. I found myself living life on life's terms instead of living life on God's terms, and it challenged everything in me. I knew what was expected of me as husband and father: secure a 9-to-5 job with great benefits and a retirement plan, work that job for 30 years and ease into retirement. But I didn't feel that was the path God had for me. I didn't want to settle into a life of everyone else's expectations and miss what God purposed for me. I wanted to live life on God's terms.

Ministry opportunities opened for me. I founded Heirs Ministries, an evangelistic team that ministered in correctional institutions, and we saw many people give their lives to the Lord. My musical gift opened doors, and in 1983, I recorded my first live gospel album. As wonderful as all that was, I knew there was so much more for me.

In my pursuit of a deeper relationship with the Lord, I recognized that we needed a different diet of the Word. So, in 1986, our family began worshiping at Rhema Christian Center in Columbus. I believe God sovereignly moved us, not only because Rhema was a Word of Faith church, but also because He was setting the stage for my future in ministry and He was maturing me as a man. I was introduced to the men's ministry of Dr. Edwin Louis Cole through his Christian Men's Network. His ministry and teachings challenged me to become the man, husband, and father God called me to be. It has helped me to this day. I was also introduced to praise and worship at Rhema. Lafayette Scales, the pastor, believed in me and invested in me. I am forever grateful to the Lord for that. At Rhema, I met Kent Henry, an incredible musician, songwriter, worship leader, and recording artist who had been invited to do a weekend worship seminar. His ministry impacted me greatly. Before the weekend ended, Kent spoke prophetically to me, telling me God would raise me to lead and teach on worship and I would travel to the nations.

> *The you that is hearing the word is not the you who will live it out. You are being prepared for its manifestation.*

It was an encouraging word but a challenging one for me. Nothing in my world matched what God had spoken. Nothing! Go to the nations? In light of my reality, that seemed unlikely. I was just trying to feed and care for my family. Maybe you've been in similar seasons—seasons of contradiction. The Lord speaks a word to you, but everything in your life contradicts that word and challenges your faith. You look at your circumstances and can't imagine how the word will become a reality. If you're not careful, you reject or reduce the word. I've learned over the years that you must receive a prophetic word, even though it makes little sense in the moment or you struggle to see it. The you who is hearing the word is not the you who will live it out. You are being prepared for its manifestation.

We all, like Abraham, will enter seasons of contradictions, but God has a way of helping us in those seasons. For me, it was the opportunity to attend the International Worship Institute (IWI) in Dallas, Texas. Rhema sent me to IWI, and once again, I knew God had sovereignly ordered my steps. Being in that environment, surrounded by songwriters, musicians, and worship leaders from around the world who were doing what God had spoken to me, allowed me to see the possibilities. My faith was ignited, and I was able to embrace the prophetic word, despite the contradictions. I still didn't know *how* God would do it, but now I could see beyond my circumstances and believe for more.

Speaking Faith-Filled Words

Life was challenging for us. By 1987, Marissa and I had five small children, and I was doing everything I knew to care for my family. Deep inside, I knew that I wasn't experiencing God's best for us. I was still learning how to be a husband and father. I'd seen the possibilities, and I never stopped confessing that there was more, that there was better. I continued to serve at Rhema, I continued to lead worship, I continued to write music, and I continued with evangelistic ministry. During that season, I wrote my first book, *The Second Flood: The Discipline of Worship*. I did what I knew to do to remain faithful to the call.

> *Your words have power. Your words build constructs. And the Word of God spoken from your mouth can shift and establish things.*

There will be many times in this process when your day-to-day reality seems inconsistent with the promises of God. God allows those inconsistencies to test and build your faith. One of the ways you strengthen your faith is by speaking faith-filled words. Your words have power. Your words build constructs, and the Word of God spoken from your mouth can shift and establish things. We read in Job 22:28: *"You will also decree a thing, and it will be established for you; And light will shine on your ways."* If you continue to speak with confidence what God has shown you, continue to confess what He has spoken to you, continue to speak faith-filled words, your faith will be strengthened.

What do I mean by faith-filled Words?

Faith-filled words are words spoken that are in line with the Word of God or words spoken directly from the Word of God. They are positive words spoken with an expectation and anticipation that allows room for God to move as He wills. They are words that ring with confidence that God is able to work in any situation, regardless of its complexity, appearance or predicted outcome. Faith-filled words are words of hope, joy, peace, love, and life!

In times of contradiction, you must remain mindful of what you speak.

There is a process that enables and empowers us to live in the realm of ridiculous faith. Sometimes the best demonstration of our faith is remaining faithful to the call, doing what we know to do while continually speaking words of faith, trusting the process, and knowing that things will shift for us in God's timing.

Chapter Three

Did I Really Hear from God?

Therefore, do not throw away your confidence, which has a great reward. For you have need of endurance, so that when you have done the will of God, you may receive what was promised.
Hebrews 10:35,36

God has spoken. He has given you a glimpse of what He has for you. He has shared His dream for you, and it is greater than anything you could dream for yourself. It's a bit overwhelming, but you have responded with a resounding "Yes!" You are doing all you know to do to remain faithful and obedient. And yet, nothing seems to be happening. Life, with all its challenges, is the antithesis of the word you've received. Years have passed. Nothing seems to change; perhaps they even have gotten worse. Now you're questioning if you've done the right thing and, little by little, doubt creeps in.

I believe most of us go through times like that as we endeavor to live in this new place of ridiculous faith. I've been there, thinking I am doing all I know in response to the prophetic words I've received, and yet not seeing those words manifest in my life. It seemed as if I was in a holding pattern, a kind of prophetic pause, and I had questions. "Why, Lord? When, Father?" And, yes, I'd begun to doubt and think, "I don't need to hear one more word about what God is going to do in and through my life!"

There will be times you feel you are in a spiritual holding pattern, but that is not the time to discard the promise. We read in Isaiah 55:11 that God's word will not return to Him without accomplishing its purpose. It will succeed. We must recognize that God is not only performing His Word *for* you; He is also performing it *in* you so He can do what He has purposed to do *through* you. The process of preparation is continual. You must learn to recognize the season you are in and steward the prophetic words you've received.

It may be a season of waiting while God moves on other fronts, preparing the way for you. It may be a season in which God desires to do a more profound work in you. He may want to reveal areas in your life where your thinking, perception, speech, and actions are not aligned with His Word. It may be that there are practical steps He is asking you to take. I do not believe that He wants to release things we are ill-prepared to steward well. This is an integral part of the process if we are to live in the realm of ridiculous faith and see God's promises realized in our lives. We must posture ourselves to hear what God requires of us that will bring forth fruit in years to come.

> *We must recognize that God is not only performing His Word for you; He is also performing it in you so that He can do what He has purposed to do through you*

Make the Adjustments

"To the degree that you are willing to discipline your life is the degree to which I will do what I've shown you," the Lord spoke to me one day in 1988. I was attending a Christian International Conference in Florida and wanted to use the time for the Lord to help me understand where I'd found myself. I had taken with me a copy of Frank Damazio's *The Making of a Leader* and was reading through the chapter on the tests that prepare us for leadership. As I prayed in my hotel room, God said to me, *"I'll show you the tests you've passed and the ones you've not."* And then He told me to develop greater discipline in my life.

I thought I led a fairly disciplined life. I was disciplined in my worship life, my prayer life, and with my time in the Word, but the Lord helped me see that I needed greater levels of discipline in other areas. If I were to launch out into full-time ministry, I'd need to shift my mindset from employee to employer; I'd need discipline in budgeting and stewarding my resources; I'd need greater discipline in time management, just to name a few. I see now that the disciplines I developed then prepared me for what I am doing now. What I didn't realize was I'd need that new level of discipline sooner than I'd thought.

At times, we may believe there are areas in our lives where we are doing fine, but God is calling us to up our game. One dear friend of mine calls it "going pro." God knows what we need to fulfill the call and complete our Kingdom assignment. It's not just about the moment we're in; the Lord sees what is down the road. He knows what we need to establish in our lives now, both spiritually and naturally, in preparation for what's to come. If you find yourself in a season of waiting, seek God and make the changes He may be requiring.

A life of ridiculous faith is one of cooperating with the Word. Yes, we pray, but we also have a responsibility to do the practical things, whether it's managing our money better, managing our time better, taking control of our health, reconciling broken relationships, or purging our homes. Sometimes what the Lord requires of us seems so small, and we can't see the connection with the vision He has given us. But whether you understand or not, your obedience is a faith response. Trust that as you obey, you are setting the stage for the next great thing God has for you.

> *"To the degree that you are willing to discipline your life is the degree to which I will do what I've shown you."*

I returned home from the CI conference and did all I knew to do to discipline my life to greater degrees. I was working for a labor union, caring for my family, and serving at Rhema. One evening in February 1989, I received a call from my friend, Robert Gay, a worship leader, recording artist with Integrity Music, and a prophet in the Body of Christ.

"I believe the Lord gave me a word for you," he said after we'd exchanged pleasantries. "I see you like a rocket on a launching pad, and you're going be launched into full-time ministry. When that happens, you're not going to have to take a cut in pay. God is going to launch you into ministry, and you are going to be able to do the things that are in your heart to do…"

Around the same time, a woman named Charlene I had met in

Dallas at IWI came to a conference at Rhema. We'd stayed in touch from the time we'd met, and she expressed an interest in sowing into Heirs Ministries. Marissa and I went to visit her in Michigan, and I shared the vision for Heirs. In June, after several conversations, she invited me to her home. She sowed a significant amount of money into Heirs Ministries—significant enough that I was able to come off my job.

"I'm going into full-time ministry," I told the director on the day I submitted my resignation. We'd established a great rapport, and he said that I could work from the same office if I needed office space. I took off two weeks and returned to the office as president of Heirs International Ministries.

I was beginning to see the fulfillment of God's word in my life. I was working to further the ministry. I completed a recording project and finished my first book. I began traveling to connect with other ministries and individuals to establish Heirs beyond Columbus and the surrounding areas. When we are willing to make the adjustments that the Lord is calling us to make in faith—no matter how small those adjustments may seem to be—we begin to see the favor of God manifest in our lives in greater and greater measure. The resources we need to walk out purpose are released. God honors our faith, faithfulness, and obedience. When we see Him move as He has promised, our faith increases even more, and we can believe for the more. We are moving into that realm of ridiculous faith.

There will be, nonetheless, greater challenges that test our faith and our resolve. Things seemed to be moving in my life. And then…

The Point of Decision
Salary, recording, traveling, and publishing a book all took resources. By the end of the year, I'd depleted my funds. I'd believe to have ongoing financial support from Charlene and others but soon discovered that would not be the case. My generous benefactor seemed to have vanished, and now I had to make some decisions for the sake of my wife and our five young children. I prayed and considered all my options, which in the natural seemed limited. I knew I could go back to the labor union job, but I wasn't sure that's what God was saying. I wanted to be sure that I didn't make a choice out of a place of fear or

simply because it was the expected, sensible thing to do. This was yet another invitation to step into the realm of ridiculous faith.

Maybe you've been in that place. Perhaps you're there right now. You've stepped out in faith and then hit a wall. Things were going well. God was moving, and it looked like you were right in sync with His purposes and plans for your life. Then the unimaginable strikes. Things take a turn you hadn't seen coming, nor had you planned for. Things get tight; it's a struggle. And you have to make some hard decisions. You are not alone. I can only imagine how Abraham felt, accepting the invitation to an adventure of faith with God only to find himself in a famine in the very land that God had promised him. He might have thought, "I didn't see this coming. I was sure we'd be well provided for in the land. Now what?" And as he weighed his options, returning to Ur was probably among them.

We all face 'Now what?' moments when we choose to move into the realm of ridiculous faith, things don't go as expected, and we are uncertain about our next move. Believe me, there will be ample opportunity to return to what you know, to choose what is convenient at the moment, to do what seems most logical or reasonable. Uncertainty comes—uncertainty about what we heard the Lord say, uncertainty about the choices we made, uncertainty that God even spoke to us.

> *Uncertainty can lead to reservation, hesitation, and retreating to that which is comfortable and familiar. We must resist the temptation to return.*

Uncertainty can lead to reservation, hesitation, and retreating to that which is comfortable and familiar. We must resist the temptation to return. We must not be quick to choose the convenient or even logical option. Still yourself, wait on God and let Him answer the question: "Now what?" He may be inviting you to stay with Him, to allow His Word to be your foundation and His Presence to be your source of strength and peace. He may be allowing the situation to teach you something more of His faithfulness, so you see Him as your real source.

You and I will always have an opportunity to draw back. Before we act, we must be still and listen for the voice of God. We must stay until He says otherwise, trusting He is working something in us that will strengthen our resolve and trust in Him.

Chapter Four

Obedience at All Cost

These have come so that the proven genuineness of your faith—of greater worth than gold, which perishes even though refined by fire—may result in praise, glory and honor when Jesus Christ is revealed.
1 Peter 1:6 NIV

The realm of ridiculous faith is a realm that assaults the logical, challenges the practical, resists the reasonable, defies the definitive, confounds the comfortable, and staggers the stability of the status quo.

The Bible is replete with examples of those who learned that cooperating with the Word of God often meant operating from this awareness, and so must you and I. We must resist our natural inclination to conform to the world's way of thinking. We must be transformed by the renewing of our minds so that all we think, speak and do is in line with the Kingdom of God, not the world's systems. At various junctures in our walk, the Lord will speak to us, instructing us to do something that may be the most illogical thing under the circumstances—something that others will not understand, something *you* may not even understand. Ridiculous faith is a faith that trusts and obeys, even if we don't fully understand why.

Will You Stay?

By the end of 1989, I was facing a 'Now what?' I had a family to care for, and I had no visible means of support. I knew I would have a job should I choose to go back to the familiar. And of course, under the circumstances, that was the most logical and responsible thing to do. But I wanted to hear from the Lord.

One day, I visited my friend Keith, a gentleman who worked in Heirs International Ministries with me. "John," he said, "I have a scripture to share with you." And he read Hebrews 10: 35-38:

Therefore, do not throw away your confidence, which has a great reward. For you have need of endurance, so that when you have done the will of God, you may receive what was promised. For yet in a very little while, He who is coming will come, and will not delay. But My righteous one shall live by faith; And if he shrinks back, My soul has no pleasure in him.

> *The realm of ridiculous faith is a realm that assaults the logical, challenges the practical, resists the reasonable, defies the definitive, confounds the comfortable, and staggers the stability of the status quo.*

The words resonated deep in my spirit. Was God speaking to me? Was He extending another invitation to live in the realm of ridiculous faith?

Later that day, I was with another friend, Juan, who was also a part of the ministry. "There's something I want to share with you," he said, and he shared the same passage of scripture. God *was* speaking, and I believed He was saying, "Don't shrink back! Stay here! Don't go down to Egypt. Stay here, and I will bless you." It was an opportunity for me to begin to exercise my faith in ways I had not before.

God had spoken to Isaac, instructing him to do something that seemed completely illogical. Isaac, the one through whom God would fulfill the covenant promised He'd made to Abraham, found himself in a famine—just like his father had. Every generation deals with the same or similar circumstances. In times of distress, lack, and uncertainty, God is looking for those who will trust Him despite the current conditions and allow Him to show His covenant through them.

We read in Genesis 26:2-3:

> *The Lord appeared to him and said, "Do not go down to Egypt; stay in the land of which I shall tell you. Sojourn in this land and I will be with you and bless you, for to you and to your descendants I will give all these lands, and I will establish the oath which I swore to your father Abraham. I will multiply your descendants as the stars of heaven, and will give your descendants all these lands; and by your descendants all the nations of the earth shall be blessed; because Abraham obeyed Me and kept My charge, My commandments, My statutes and My laws."*

Isaac had a family and men for whom he was responsible; it would make sense to go where sustenance was available. But the Lord instructed him to stay in the land, even though there was a famine. He explicitly told Isaac not to go down to Egypt, with the promise that He would bless him as He'd blessed Abraham. God wanted Isaac to learn to trust Him completely and to know Him as his sole source of provision. The Lord was inviting Isaac into the realm of ridiculous faith to demonstrate His faithfulness to honor His word.

> *In times of distress, lack, and uncertainty, God is looking for those who will trust Him despite the current conditions and allow Him to show His covenant through them.*

God honors the faithfulness of those who serve Him. His intention is that His Word and His blessings be passed from one generation to the next. He desires the manifestation of His Word, His Power, His Presence, His Provision, His Covenant would be greater than in the preceding generation (Deuteronomy 6, 7:6-9). This was what He wanted to teach Isaac, and by Isaac's example, teach us.

> *God desires that manifestation of His Word, His Power, His Presence, His Provision, His Covenant would be greater than in the preceding generation.*

As we continue to read, we see that Isaac sowed in the land (v.12a). How illogical is that? Who sows in ground that, to the natural eye, cannot produce? I can imagine people watching him, thinking he was crazy for wasting perfectly good seed. Did he really expect a harvest? Sowing was an act of faith. God had spoken, "Stay, and I'll bless you." Isaac had an expectation, and he sowed. We read that he reaped a hundredfold in the same year! Ridiculous faith had produced ridiculous results! God wants to do the same for you and me.

Now Isaac sowed in that land and reaped in the same year a hundredfold. And the Lord blessed him, and the man became rich, and continued to grow richer until he became very wealthy; for he had possessions of flocks and herds and a great household, so that the Philistines envied him (Genesis 26:12-14).

I now had the same opportunity to trust God.

I admit it was challenging. I wasn't traveling; I wasn't doing a lot in ministry as I'd expected. And, unfortunately, I had allowed an offense to cause me to leave Rhema, the place where God taught me, matured me, and blessed me. I'm sure others were looking at me, thinking I was being irresponsible. Well-meaning individuals would say, "It didn't work, John. Maybe it's not time. Can you get your job back?" I could, but I believed I was where God wanted me to be. I didn't want to go back to what I'd done before with the attitude of, "Well, at least, I tried it, and it just didn't work." So until God spoke, I would remain with Him in this place.

Often, as we learn to navigate this new realm of faith, we step out in obedience, and we may not readily see the fruit of our obedience. We will step out, but we will not always stick it out. We may never know what we miss because we are not willing to stay out there. Living in the realm of ridiculous faith will require that we learn to wait, to endure some things. Isaac didn't see the harvest in an instant. And while the Bible doesn't tell us what was going on in Isaac's world between the time of sowing and the time of reaping, I can imagine it was a challenging season. But he remained! You and I must be willing to do the same.

Opportunities opened up for me. The assistant secretary of a small church on the west side of Columbus informed me that the church needed someone to lead worship. They gave me a small offering that helped during this season. But it was still a challenging time for us, and at one point, I even had to apply for public assistance. I'd get up, put on a suit and tie, go to the welfare office and wait in the long lines, all the while believing that things were going to turn around. I know this sounds crazy, but I just did not want to miss God. I was standing on God's promise in Philippians 4:19: *"And my God will supply all your needs according to His riches in glory in Christ Jesus."* I'd continually say, "It will not always be like this."

We live in a society that makes it easy *not* to walk by faith. The programs designed to help us have their place and supply some support and benefits, but if we are not careful, they can keep us from exercising our faith to a greater degree. I was willing to do what I needed to do to care for my family in that season because I knew it was only temporary. God would honor His word as long as I continued to trust Him and obey His voice.

The Fruit of Obedience

That season lasted for two years. After receiving another prophetic word, I felt a release to talk with the labor union director and get my job back. The word came through my friend, Terri. "John," she said, "the Lord knows your heart's desire to walk in faith. He also knows the needs of your family. It is not a lack of faith to go back to a job." I knew that was God. I wept with relief. I felt I had passed the test of obedience. I called my previous employer, and he created a position for me. *Created a position!* That's the favor of God. My new job required that I travel, and I didn't have a car. "John needs a car," the pastor of the small church where I was serving told one of the members. This gentleman owned an auto repair shop with his brother. He called a dealership and found a Pontiac Sunbird. After checking it out and putting new tires on it, they *gave* me the car.

Before launching out into full-time ministry, I had written a song, "Under the Shadow." Worship leader, Kent Henry had heard the chorus, asked if he could add a verse and record it. Integrity Music listened to the song, reached out to me and asked to record and publish it. That was the first published song to create revenue for my family. My first royalty check was $.98 (which I still have as a memorial); the next was over $5,000. I was now getting a glimpse of God providing for us through the music that He blessed me to write. My music was now touching the world.

To an onlooker, those two years may have looked like I'd missed God or had misinterpreted what I heard. I never felt that way. God did bless us. He continued to provide for us, and I learned valuable lessons. I learned how to find strength in suffering. I also learned about what the Apostle Paul calls the "obedience of faith" (Romans 1:5; 16:26). There may be times that God will call us to obey in order to test our faith. This is a time of proving, and you must expect that these tests will come. If you can stay where He has you rather than abort the process, you will see the fruit of your obedience on the other side of the test. You may not see the fruit in the moment, but it will come. Our willingness to suffer for the sake of the call and act in obedience at all costs produces a harvest, and for me it was a harvest that I'd see for years to come.

Chapter Five

Ridiculous Faith: Some Movement Required

Now faith is the assurance of things hoped for, the conviction of things not seen. For by it the men of old gained approval.
Hebrews 11:1-2

Ridiculous faith will create the opportunity for ridiculous favor, ridiculous resources, and ridiculous harvest. God will do incredible things in our lives when we are willing to let go of the rational approach to life and allow Holy Spirit to lead us into new realms of faith. He wants to demonstrate the power of His Kingdom to us and through us. We must remain attentive to the voice of God and be willing to go where Holy Spirit is leading us.

With each invitation the Lord extends to live in the realm of ridiculous comes an opportunity to develop a greater level of faith that will allow us to see God move in unprecedented ways in our lives. You and I must resolve to act in faith, even when it challenges our sense of reason. God often gives illogical instructions which ultimately lead to miraculous results. We must be willing to obey, even if we look foolish to others.

Time to Move

While I was working for the labor union, the Lord made it clear that what He had for me was not in Columbus, and He would be moving us. I shared this with Marissa, and as an act of faith, we began looking for that next place. This was a deliberate choice to act in faith. God had spoken. We believed His Word and demonstrated that belief by our actions, believing that as we looked, the Lord would reveal the next place He had for us. I believed that as I acted in faith, doors of opportunity would open. And they did.

> *Ridiculous faith will create the opportunity for ridiculous favor, ridiculous resources, and ridiculous harvest.*

My involvement in leading worship, songwriting, and speaking at worship seminars and workshops created opportunities for us. I was soon invited by two pastors to join the staff at their churches; I decided to visit both. The first visit was to Richland, North Carolina, to meet with Dr. Kelley Varner. The other trip was to Houma, Louisiana. There I met with Pastor Jules Boquet. Both pastors knew of my ministry as a worship leader and knew of my music. When I returned home, I told Marissa I felt Louisiana was the place God had for us. So we made a trip there together. We had a wonderful time with Pastor Boquet and his wife. Jules had made me a great offer, considering the meager means we'd been living with, and I had decided to accept. But as Marissa and I prayed and researched the area—especially the school system—we weren't sure that Louisiana would be the best place for our children.

As we considered our options, I received a call from a friend, David Wright. Dave was a music pastor of a church in Middletown, Ohio, just north of Cincinnati.

"Hey, John," he said. "I was wondering if you looked into the church in Cincinnati that I told you about." Dave had mentioned this church to me about six months earlier, but I wasn't interested.

> *God often gives illogical instructions which ultimately lead to miraculous results. We must be willing to obey, even if we look foolish to others.*

The truth was I was still harboring offense after leaving Rhema; the idea of working in a church I felt to be similar was not appealing. Whenever we look at life through the lens of offense, we cannot see through the eyes of faith. Offense skews our vision and can cause us to miss the next thing, the next place God has for us in the fulfillment of purpose and destiny.

"No, Dave, I didn't. I wasn't interested."

"I really think you should," he continued. "I think it is an exact fit for you, and they haven't found anybody yet."

I decided, as a courtesy to Dave, to call.

The Act of Faith

The Bible is filled with examples of men and women who acted in faith. We read in Hebrews 11 that the act of faith gained these men and women approval and pleased God. They were commended for their acts of faith! One translation says they "obtained a good report." The Message Bible puts it this way:

> *The fundamental fact of existence is that this trust in God, this faith, is the firm foundation under everything that makes life worth living. It's our handle on what we can't see. <u>The act of faith is what distinguished our ancestors, set them above the crowd</u>* (Hebrews 11:1,2, emphasis added).

And it will distinguish us from others as well! This faith journey is one of cooperation. That's what the Apostle James tells us in his epistle when he writes that *"faith without works is dead."* God will speak. Our faith in His ability and His faithfulness to fulfill His Word causes us to act. He may be speaking to you about going back to school. Your act of faith is to look into programs and fill out applications. Perhaps He is speaking to you about changing your career or changing location. You demonstrate your faith by taking steps in that direction, trusting that as you move, He will bring clarity or, if necessary, redirection. As you move, doors will open for you, information will become available to you, and you'll find yourself walking in unprecedented favor.

> *The act of faith is an action taken as a direct result of a decision to totally trust and act on God's Word despite one's limited ability or complete inability to see, reason, or comprehend.*

What is the Act of Faith?

- *It is an action taken as a direct result of a decision to totally trust and act on God's Word despite one's limited*

ability or complete inability to see, reason, or comprehend.
- *It is an action taken in absolute confidence that God is able to accomplish what He has spoken regardless of its complexity or seeming impossibility.*
- *It is an action taken with the belief that at the very moment the decision is made that which God has spoken is done. Once acted upon, everything needed to fulfill it is in motion, and the desired outcome is assured.*

Walking through the Door

The moment we say yes to God, things happen. As we act in faith, doors will open. But every door of opportunity that opens is not necessarily the door God desires us to walk through. That is why it is essential we listen for God's voice every step of the way and ask Him to shut any doors we are not to walk through—no matter how inviting it may be. I had prayed just that.

It is also important to know that as God opens doors of opportunity, there may come opposition from the enemy to keep you from moving forward. Right at the time I'd said I would look into the opportunity in Cincinnati, a man driving recklessly down our street, slammed into our van and knocked the van into our car. The van was totaled, and the car, while still drivable, had a big dent in the rear bumper. The driver hadn't stopped, and we had no insurance on either vehicle at the time. We were able to track the driver down, but he didn't have any insurance either. While I was discouraged for a few days, I regained my focus and continued to press forward in faith. You and I must not quit when opposition comes. See it as an opportunity to exercise your faith in greater measure and continue to trust God to fulfill His Word!

I called Christ Emmanuel Christian Fellowship (CECF) in Cincinnati, as I'd told Dave I would, and spoke with the pastor, Michael E. Dantley. They invited me to Cincinnati, and I called Pastor Jules to let him know I was reconsidering his offer. He immediately pulled the offer, closing that door. The position at CECF had not been filled after six months, and I believed God had left it open for me.

I drove to Cincinnati and met with Pastor (now Bishop) Dantley, his wife, Carol, and Bennie Fluellen, the associate pastor. I knew this was the open door I was to walk through. We moved to Cincinnati in June of 1992, and I joined Christ Emmanuel's staff as the Pastor of Music Worship and Arts. God also opened a door that allowed us to rent a home, and our children were able to attend school in one of the best districts in the state.

Those years at CECF were some of my most fruitful and productive years of ministry. God did amazing things through the music ministry. He connected me with some of the most gifted and talented people I've ever met and knitted our hearts together. The Lord also continued to mature me, prune me, and prepare me. He was working in me, doing things in me that would remain with me forever.

Lay It on the Altar
"One day for each year of your life."
These are the words I heard the Lord speak to me, calling me to a fast. I was 36 years old, and while fasting wasn't foreign to me, I had never fasted that long. I was to start the fast on Saturday, January 1, 1994. I chose not to. The next day, after the first Sunday morning service, one of our worship team members asked if she could speak with me. She handed me a piece of paper. "This is what God spoke to me this morning concerning you. He told me to give it to you." I read it, and though I can't recall exactly what it said, I can tell I did not eat for the next 36 days. The Lord was drawing me to a place in Him that I'd never been before. He will continually invite us to those places to know Him more intimately, to become more of who He created us to be, and to enable and empower us to walk in greater levels of faith.

> **God will continually invite us to those places to know Him more intimately, to become more of who He created us to be, and to enable and empower us to walk in greater levels of faith.**

Those 36 days changed my life. The Lord had said, *"During these 36 days, I want you to study My Word concerning My glory and the Fire of God."* I decided not to pray about my future in music or anything like that. I studied the Word and I sought God.

At the time of my fast, Christ Emmanuel was preparing for their first recording project. A month after I'd ended the fast, we recorded a night of live worship. I cannot begin to describe what an incredible evening it was! It encapsulated everything I'd always envisioned, and I knew something special had taken place with the recording of *Nation of Praise*. God had breathed on it; He had blessed it and would use it to bless many. I stepped off the platform, thinking this was just the beginning. Then I heard God say, *"This season for you is over."*

I immediately thought, "This *can't* be God! Not after what just happened here!" But I knew He was speaking. He was asking me to lay it down now, and it was not just walking away from Christ Emmanuel, but laying everything down on the altar and trusting Him with it all.

I had been intentional during the fast not to pray about music and worship. I said to the Lord, "I'm grateful for everything You've done for me in music and worship. If that season is over for me, I'm OK with that as long as I have Your Presence." And I left it all there.

We will always be tested as we endeavor to live in the realm of ridiculous faith. At some point, we will be asked to lay our "Isaacs" on the altar. Abraham, again, is our example. God had fulfilled His Word; the heir of promise had been born to Abraham after 25 years of believing. Paul tells us in Romans that Abraham did not waver but grew strong in faith, fully confident that God was able to perform that which He'd promised (Romans 4:20-21). And God did just that.

But then God speaks the words we read in Genesis 22: 2: **"Take now your son, your only son, whom you love, Isaac, and go to the land of Moriah, and offer him there as a burnt offering on one of the mountains of which I will tell you."** God was asking Abraham to offer to Him the very thing He had promised. This was a defining moment for Abraham. He had a choice. Scripture doesn't give us any indication that he debated or try to reason with God. He simply acted in faith and obedience.

You will face your own defining moments in your desire to move into greater places of faith. The Lord may ask you to surrender the very thing you believed He would use, the very gift He has given you to walk out purpose and destiny. He may ask you to move to a place that looks like a step backward, a place that looks like loss, just as you've experienced one of the greatest victories of your life. And you, too, will have a choice. God wants us to choose Him over all else—over gifts, over possessions, over ministry. This may be one of the greatest and often most challenging acts of faith.

We know how the story on Mt. Moriah ends. Just as Abraham raises the knife to slay Isaac, God halts him and says, *"Now I know! Now I know that you will not hold anything back from Me. Now I know that you trust Me with all that you are and all that you have. Now I know that I can trust you with even more."* And God promises to bless Abraham and greatly multiply his seed.

Your faith must be in the One who promises, and you must believe that on the other side of any sacrifice He asks you to make is something grander and greater than what you are surrendering. There will be multiple times as you walk with Him that you will face the choice of holding on or laying all down. It's then you must be willing to echo the words of the Apostle Paul in Philippians 3:7-8:

But whatever things were gain to me, those things I have counted as loss for the sake of Christ. More than that, I count all things to be loss in view of the surpassing value of knowing Christ Jesus my Lord, for whom I have suffered the loss of all things, and count them but rubbish so that I may gain Christ...

After the recording was mixed and mastered, we released *Nation of Praise*. It took off and was blessing people all over the world. Things were going well, and though it seemed illogical, I shared with my pastor that I believed my time at CECF was over. I laid it all down, ready to accept the next invitation into the *Realm of Ridiculous Faith*.

Chapter Six

The Next Realm of Possibilities

Now to Him who is able to do far more abundantly beyond all that we ask or think, according to the power that works within us.

Ephesians 3:20

The realm of ridiculous faith is the realm of infinite possibilities, only limited by our inability to believe that with God all things really are possible. God wants us to experience Him in His totality, to know all He can and desires to be in our lives. He invites us to partner with Him so He can reveal Himself to us.

There will be times when the circumstances and situations in our lives demand the exercising of ridiculous faith. Then there are times when Holy Spirit is looking for someone who can access that realm of faith and invite others to act in obedience to the Word of the Lord and experience the miraculous. He wants to use us to draw in those who say, "I want to go there with You! I am willing to pay the price to see the reality of Your Word in my life."

The prophet Elijah learned to live in that place, and through him, the Lord fed a widow and her son for nearly three years (1 Kings 17:8-16). Her act of faith in preparing a small cake for Elijah before making one for her son and herself allowed her to see the manifestation of God's power in her life. I can see her each day as she prepared a meal, dipping into what should have been an empty bowl and drawing out flour for each meal.

Elisha invited a widow faced with losing her children if her debt was not paid to step into this realm (2 Kings 4: 1-7). She must have looked pretty ridiculous, running to all of her neighbors' homes. "I need to borrow all the empty vessels you can spare!" She may have felt a little silly pouring what little oil she had into those vessels and expecting them to be filled. But as she obeyed the word of the Lord through the prophet, each vessel was filled with oil—enough oil to pay off the debt and for her and children to live on. Ridiculous!

> *The realm of ridiculous faith is the realm of infinite possibilities, only limited by our inability to believe that with God all things really are possible.*

But no more ridiculous than the many instructions Jesus gave to His disciples, teaching them to live in this realm of faith by feeding the multiple with five loaves of bread and two fish (Matthew 14:14-21). Or telling Peter to go the sea, cast in a hook, take the first fish that he caught, for in its mouth would be just enough to pay their taxes (Matthew 17:24-27). He is calling you and me to participate with Him the same way.

You see, it's not just about you and your purpose and destiny. It's also about the legacy of faith you leave for those coming behind you—your children, your grandchildren, and others who are connected to you. God wants them to see through you the amazing possibilities that exist in His Kingdom for all who will exercise ridiculous faith. He is the same God who provided for the widows, who fed the multitudes, who provided resources for the disciples, and so much more.

> *It's not just about you and your purpose and destiny. It's also about the legacy of faith you leave for those coming behind you—your children, your grandchildren, and others who are connected to you.*

Stepping into the "Next"

I stepped off the platform at Christ Emmanuel Christian Fellowship that evening in 1994, only knowing one thing: God had spoken, and a new adventure of faith was about to begin. My "yes" to God was my acceptance of another invitation to a new place of faith. Not only would the next place test and mature me, but my children would begin to learn, at an early age, what faith in God can do.

God opened a door through the owner of Destiny Image Publishing, Don Nori. I had published two books through Destiny Image and had had the privilege of leading worship for one of Don's meetings in Shippensburg, Pennsylvania. In the course of a conversation, he'd asked if I'd consider moving to Shippensburg to work with him at Destiny Image—something I never imagined myself doing. After sharing that conversation with my wife and the leaders at Christ Emmanuel, I decided to travel to Shippensburg and meet with Don. I believed this was the move God wanted us to make. It wasn't a move that we had planned for, and I knew we would have to trust God every step of the way.

"We're moving!" I announced when I got home, and we began the process. I had chatted with the gentleman who drove me to the airport to catch my flight back home. "If you're moving here," he'd said, "you'll need a place to live. You want to build a house? I can give you the name of a builder who can work with you." So I reached out to the builder.

"We don't have any money saved up for a house," I told him.

"Well, I tell you what I'll do," he said. "I will build the house and finance it for you. Can you come up with $5,000 for a down payment on a $150,000 home?"

"I don't have $5000, but I have faith for it. Give me 30 days!" I told him.

I shared our plans with Pastor Dantley, and he went to the CECF family. "John's going to be leaving," he announced. "We want to bless them as they go."

They received an offering for our family—roughly $7,000!

The Backside of the Desert

Shippensburg is a small borough in south-central Pennsylvania with a population today of just under 6,000. Stepping into this town is like stepping into a different time in history. Main Street was dotted with small shops run by the owners. No one ever seemed to be in a hurry, and on any given Sunday morning, you might drive behind a horse and buggy as a Mennonite family made their way to church.

The town was so small that if anyone new moved there, just about everyone knew about it. Our family experienced culture shock when we arrived, and I think it was a bit of a shock to the community as well. We were one of the few African American families in the town and were by far the largest one. There was some speculation as to where we had come from and what had brought us there. For the most part, however, the people were cordial, and we made some friends that we still have today.

For a short time, I commuted between Shippensburg and Cincinnati. We didn't want to disrupt the children in the middle of the school year. The house we were having built had not been completed, but I wanted my family with me once school ended. I began looking, with no success, for a temporary home that would accommodate seven people. There was a brand-new, empty house up the street from our soon-to-be new home.

"I'm trying to find a place to move into until our house is finished," I mentioned to the builder, who lived in the same subdivision where we would soon live.

"Call your family," he told me. "Tell them you found a place. I'll rent the house up the street to you until your house is complete."

God moved so our family could be together. This was just one of the many ways He proved Himself to our family during that season. We saw His favor, and it was just the beginning. If you and I are to live in the realm of ridiculous faith, we will, at some point, find ourselves in places where all we have to rely on is God and God alone. I had yet to realize that was, in part, what this season of my life would teach us all.

Our time in Shippensburg was not exactly as I'd expected it to be, and I have found when following the Lord and walking by faith, things rarely ever are. I think of those years as my "backside of the desert" period. It was a different kind of challenge for my family and me in so many ways. My title at Destiny Image was Director of Author Relations, and I worked closely with the top authors who were a part of the company's catalog. I was learning so much in a completely new arena for me. I felt totally out of my element, and it played with my confidence. The truth is, I felt incompetent. I was trying to fit into a system that I wasn't equipped for, and one for which I wasn't wired.

Once I was able to utilize my skills as a negotiator, I felt I was more of an asset to the company.

It was part of the process. I recognized there was a deeper work the Lord wanted to do in me in preparation for the next stage of ministry. I wasn't doing a lot in music while in Shippensburg, other than playing for Don's small congregation. I realized how much I had allowed what I did musically to become a part of my identity. I admit that it bothered me that nobody knew who I was or what I had done. They would play music in the office—music I'd written—and no one had a clue. I wanted to shout, "I wrote that song!" but I couldn't. I've learned that to live in the realm of ridiculous faith, we must be secure in who we are in Christ and get our affirmation from God alone. We do not find our identity in our gifts and talents but in Him. When God begins to speak to us concerning the "ridiculous" things He has purposed to do in and through us, others may not always be able to see it. If their affirmation is vital to us and we don't receive it, we won't step out, we won't grow, and we won't experience the great—and ridiculous—things God has purposed for us.

> *To live in the realm of ridiculous faith, we must be secure in who we are in Christ and get our affirmation from God alone.*

My assignment with Destiny Image didn't last long. After a year of working there, it became apparent that it wasn't working for the company or me. Things began to change, and I knew I couldn't continue to work there. "I think I need to resign," I told Marissa, and she agreed. Destiny Image and I parted on amicable terms, and for the remainder of our time in Shippensburg, God moved miraculously on our behalf.

Just at the time I resigned from Destiny Image, doors opened to lead and teach on worship around the country. I was stepping back into itinerate ministry, and we only had one vehicle. One day, I'd gone to Destiny Image; I'd needed to complete some paperwork. As I pulled into the parking lot, I noticed a Mercedes Benz parked there. It was an older model, but it was in mint condition.

"Who does that Mercedes belong to?" I asked some of the employees. I found out it belonged to the mother of one of the editors, Julie

Martin. I spoke to her about the car and she, in turn, spoke to her father. She told him I was interested in it. Now, I had just resigned from my job, so purchasing an automobile was the last thing on my mind.

"You like the car," Marissa said. "There's no harm in inquiring about it."

"What are your plans for the ministry? What is your vision?" Julie's father, Jim, asked when I called him. Julie had told him I was in ministry and was going to be traveling. He asked me if we had a 501c3, which we did, and then said he'd get back with me.

"I'll tell you what I'm going to do," Jim said when he called a few days later. "I'm not going to sell you the car. I'm going to give it to you. It belongs to my wife, and she wants to trade it in. I've made arrangements with the owner of the dealership to sell the car to you."

He asked me to meet him and gave me the time and location. When we met, he wrote a check to the ministry for the price of the car, and then I wrote a check to purchase the car. God had provided the transportation that allowed me to travel for a year. During that year, I watched the Lord do incredible things in our family, drawing us closer together, strengthening our faith. It was a year of learning to trust God and see Him move in a greater way. He was preparing me for my next assignment. I saw the reality of His Word—*with God, nothing is impossible.*

Chapter 7

Transitions, Transitions, Transitions

And looking at them Jesus said to them, "With people this is impossible, but with God all things are possible."
Matthew 19:26

Transitions! I heard in my spirit in January of 1997, and I told my wife and children that we'd be moving again. I didn't know where, but I was sure we would move before the year ended. I'd soon learn that "transition" would not just apply to a geographic move but also to things much more eternal.

Change and transition are a part of life; they are inevitable. We come to expect them. But knowing they will come doesn't necessarily make it easy when they do come. There are some changes we welcome. We've prayed for them; we embrace them. Then there are other times when change and transition uproot and disrupt everything. We struggle with them; we may even resist them. We will discuss change and transition in more detail in Chapter 13, but for now, we must understand that God uses transition to transform us and to guide us to the place He ultimately has for us. If we trust Him, listen attentively to His voice, and obey, even when we may be challenged in the transition, we will see His provision and can experience His peace.

Throughout their history, the children of Israel experienced many transitions. God sovereignly led Jacob, his sons and their families to Egypt to preserve their lives during a famine. There they multiplied and grew strong. Then God led them out of Egypt, out of bondage, across the Red Sea, and to Mount Sinai, where He further established His covenant, His purpose and the destiny of the nation. He gave them the Law, detailed plans for constructing the Tabernacle, and the pattern for worship. His ultimate goal was the Promised Land.

We read in Numbers 9:15-23 that the Lord led them by a cloud and a pillar of fire. When the cloud lifted from over the Tabernacle, they knew it was time to move. Those moves were not easy for Israel. They had to gather up everything in the Tabernacle—the Ark of the Covenant, the brazen altar, the altar of incense, the candlesticks, all the curtains and poles, everything—and follow the cloud. Each individual tribe had to gather their families and all their belongings to move. Sometimes the cloud only remained over the Tabernacle for a day, other times much longer. They had to keep their eyes focused on the cloud, move when it moved, and settle where it settled. Inconvenient? Absolutely! But they understood one thing: their safety, their provision, their very destiny was only assured as they moved with the cloud!

> *We must be willing to exercise our faith in the face of change and transition. Our courage to confidently advance and fulfill the will of God for our lives comes from acknowledging and accepting the reality that God is in charge!*

We must learn to move as God directs when God directs. It may, at times, be inconvenient. We may feel ill-prepared to move. We may not have everything we think we need. We may fear the unknown. We may have become quite comfortable where we are. In fact, things may be good where we are, and we see no reason to move. But we must trust the One who sees all things and knows all things concerning our lives. We must trust the One who orders our steps to guide us to the place He has prepared for us, a place of fulfillment.

We must be willing to exercise our faith in the face of change and transition. Our courage to confidently advance and fulfill the will of God for our lives comes from acknowledging and accepting the reality that God is in charge! He is working in us through transition and change, moving us in place to encounter His glory.

A Prepared Heart

"Marissa, I want to spend my father's birthday with him," I told my wife. My father's birthday was January 26, and the Lord had let me know that this birthday would be his last. He had suffered a heart attack the summer of 1995 while in his backyard, and had been rushed to the hospital. God had spared his life, and I had the opportunity of leading him to the Lord while he was still in the hospital. Shortly after that, my father was diagnosed with congestive heart failure and other ailments due to a lifestyle of bad choices. He was becoming increasingly weak as the months went by. I would drive our family to Columbus, Ohio to see him over those next two years.

I saw my father getting weaker and prayed this simple prayer, a different kind of prayer: "Father, if You are not going to heal him, don't let him suffer." So when the Lord told me that this would be his last birthday, I was not alarmed. I was grateful to know the Father loved me enough to tell me His intentions and He trusted me with this knowledge and would give me the grace to walk through it.

I drove the eight hours from Shippensburg, Pennsylvania to Columbus, Ohio on a Saturday so I could spend the following day with my father. It was a Super Bowl Sunday. Now, I am not a sports enthusiast, but it didn't matter. Whatever my dad wanted to do on that day was fine with me; I just wanted to be with him. We went to the Elks Club where some of his friends had gathered to watch the game. He introduced me to his friends—many of them I already knew. But he was so happy I had driven that distance to spend his birthday with him and he wanted everyone to know I was there. We sat and watched the game, ate, and just enjoyed the day and one another.

I am forever grateful to God for giving me that chance to create memories with my dad, to be with him on what would be his last birthday and preparing me for what was to come.

Moving with God

As the year progressed, the Lord gave us more clarity concerning our transition from Shippensburg. We still didn't know exactly where we'd be going, but as an act of faith, I began looking. Various opportunities in ministry opened up. One was with a ministry on the East coast. The salary they offered me was more than I'd ever made to lead worship. I made a trip to meet with the pastor, and they rolled out the red carpet for me. They were intentional in showing all the possibilities that awaited me there, even picking me up in a Rolls Royce for a service in which I led worship. The next day I met again with the pastor, and he told me all the things he was willing to do to move my family there.

"I don't think that is what the Lord has for us," I told Marissa when I returned to Shippensburg. It was something I could easily do, and I didn't need to exercise much faith to do it. I believed that the Lord wanted to do something different in our lives, something that would require a greater level of faith and trust in Him. One of the many things I've learned about living a life of faith is that it's a conscious decision we make over and over again. We continually grow in our faith, and we can stop growing at any point. We can simply choose not to go any further. But when we stop growing, we can miss the more God has for us! We forfeit more than we will ever know by settling for something far less than God desires.

> *Living a life of faith is a conscious decision we make over and over again. We continually grow in our faith, and we can stop growing at any point.*

Marissa and I prayed, and by faith, we put our house on the market while we waited for the Lord to give us further direction concerning our next move. During that time, the Lord began to draw us even closer together as a family of faith. As I moved more into itinerate ministry, I saw and heard more clearly what this next move was about.

> *We forfeit more than we will ever know by settling for something far less than God desires.*

It was about fulfilling destiny—not just my destiny but our destiny as a family!

From One Generation to the Next

We have seen that God desires to bless His children from generation to generation. That is why we so often read that He is the God of Abraham, Isaac, and Jacob. Children learn to live by faith and to trust God in all things by watching their parents walk out their faith. I'm convinced that God not only wants us to model a life of ridiculous faith before our children, but to include them in the process. Then they can see faith at work for themselves, and know that God responds to *their* faith. God would demonstrate to our five children His love and His provision through this move in a way that would have lasting impact.

By May of that year, our house had sold, and we prepared to move at the end of June once the children had finished the school year. After looking for a home in Columbus, we realized we weren't to move there; God was sending us back to Cincinnati. Once that was settled, we quickly found a home. However, we faced one hurdle: we were $3,500.00 short of the down payment we needed, and we were running out of time. We were scheduled to move in a couple of weeks. We needed a financial miracle.

Two weeks passed and we *had* to move by the weekend. The Wednesday before, the Lord had instructed me to have bible study with our family. So I got everyone together and told the children to bring their bibles.

"Every time we have moved," I began, "it was with a desire to follow the Lord." I showed them in Scripture how God led Joseph and Mary through various moves when Jesus was born and explained that every move they'd made fulfilled a word written about Jesus. Now, to be honest, I wasn't sure if any of it was making sense to them, but I was being obedient and following the Lord's instructions. I went on to tell them that as Jesus fulfilled His ministry, there were times when He would call forth what He needed.

"On one occasion, He needed a donkey to ride into the city to fulfill a word spoken about Him," I explained. "He didn't own a donkey, so He sent two of His disciples to a specific location and told them they would find a donkey tied up and waiting for them. Jesus said, 'Simply ask for it. Tell the owner I need it, and he will give it to you.' The men did exactly what Jesus told them to do and brought the donkey back to Him."

I shared a few other examples and further explained that these things happened for Jesus because He was fulfilling His destiny. "We are moving to fulfill our destiny, and whatever we need, we simply need to ask for it. What do we need to make this move?" I asked.

"We need patience!" one of the children said.

I laughed and thought, "OK, let's come back to that one."

"We need money!" another said.

"Yes, we need money! So here's what we're going to do," I told them. "We're going to pray right now and tell money to come to us!" We joined hands and prayed that the $3,500.00 we needed would come to us quickly. Marissa suggested we take communion. So we took some bread and Kool-Aid and had communion together. (Yes, Kool-Aid. You work with what you have, and God honors it).

Thirty minutes later, the phone rang. It was Julie, my former co-worker at Destiny Image. "Hi, John," she said. "We heard you were moving out of town, and Dad wants to know if you and your family would have a meal with us before you leave." Her father, Jim, was the businessman who had sown a car into our ministry. We agreed to meet the following evening at their family-owned restaurant.

The following morning at around 10:30, there was a knock at the door. It was a FedEx delivery man with an envelope for me. I opened it and found a card from our dear friends John and Susan Perodeau, who lived in Detroit, Michigan. Proverbs 3:27 from the Message Bible was written inside the card. It read: *"Never walk away from someone who deserves help; your hand is God's hand for that person."*

And there was a check for $2,500.00!

"Come here!" I shouted to Marissa and the children. "God is answering our prayer!" I showed them the check. We prayed and thanked the Lord.

That evening we went to dinner with the Martins and had a wonderful time. Jim asked about our plans once we moved.

"I'm not totally sure right now, but I will continue in ministry," I told him.

"Do you mind coming to our home for a few minutes?" he asked when we'd finished dinner. As we were driving towards his home, we were amazed to see the house we were going to was one we would see from the highway. We had always wondered who lived there, and now we knew. We were going to *that* house.

Once inside, the children watched the Christian music video, "The Call" by the gospel group Anointed while the adults sat and talked. At one point Jim left the room. When he returned, he made his way over to me and slipped a piece of paper in my hand. "Keep up the good work!" he said.

He'd handed me a check for $1000.00! God had answered our prayers in less than 24 hours! We had the $3,500.00 we needed to make the down payment on our new home!

I shared with Jim the prayer we had prayed the night before. He just smiled and said, "The Lord told me to do that." I thanked him and asked him to pray for our family before we left. We headed home that evening with a heightened awareness of the faithfulness of God to answer prayers. To this day, our children remember that time, and we still encourage one another all these years later that He is still the same God!

Dealing with change and transition has taught me much. We cannot be in a hurry or act in fear. We must be willing to extend our faith and wait on God, realizing:

- *When you move with God, you can expect other things (and people) to move also. He is speaking to those He will use as His instruments of blessings for you.*
- *You must expect Holy Spirit to point to areas in your life that must change in order to keep moving with God in faith. When He does, be quick to make those changes so you remain aligned with His Word and His purposes for you.*
- *You must be willing to walk through the process, no matter how challenging it may be.*
- *Moving with God will always require faith and obedience. You will find that the Lord often gives us Illogical Instructions for Miraculous Results. Trust and obey.*

By mid-July, after staying in Columbus for a couple weeks, we moved into our new home in Cincinnati. The children quickly made new friends in the neighborhood, and I sought the Lord for clarity concerning the direction I was to go in ministry.

I soon realized that more transitions were ahead as He extended another invitation to the realm of ridiculous faith.

Chapter 8

Grace in the Realm of Ridiculous Faith

> *I am crucified with Christ: nevertheless I live; yet not I, but Christ liveth in me: and the life which I now live in the flesh I live by the faith of the Son of God, who loved me, and gave himself for me.*
> Galatians 2:20 (KJV)

Someone once asked me if I ever had "Lord, I believe; help my unbelief" moments. The truth is, every time the Lord has spoken to me about doing something or has shown me what He has for me that is larger and grander than anything I've ever pictured for myself, I feel that way. So if you are feeling some level of unbelief, that's OK. You may be saying, "Yes, Lord, I believe You can do all things. I believe Your Word is true. I believe that Your Word concerning my life is true. I'm struggling with my part in this. Am I really the one? Can I really do this? I need You to help the part of me that is struggling to see what You see."

God understands that. He will help you with any areas of unbelief if you allow Him to. You simply need to acknowledge where you are. He helps you with feelings of inadequacy if you make the choice to stand in the truth of God's Word. And He will continue to do the deep work in you that prepares you to step into the place He ordained for you before the foundation of the world (Ephesians 1:4).

You and I have been called with a "holy calling" (2 Timothy 2:9). We are God's ***"workmanship, created in Christ Jesus for good works, which God prepared beforehand so that we would walk in them"***

(Ephesians 2:10). When God begins to reveal that calling, our purpose and destiny, the "good works" we are to walk in, He will always show us something far beyond anything we've ever dreamed and anything we can accomplish without Him. Often our tendency is to disqualify ourselves for a variety of reasons: our age, our perceived ability or inability, our flaws and imperfections, our past, our resources. Our inability to see in ourselves what God sees can keep us from stepping into a place of ridiculous faith.

> *God affirms you and, through His Word, your mind is transformed, and your thoughts are aligned with His thoughts.*

But God knows what He has deposited in us. He knows who we are and what we truly are capable of in Him. He wants us to trust what He already knows to be true concerning us. He wants us to submit to His will and the transformative work He desires to do in us, which prepares us to step fully into our true calling. Living in the realm of ridiculous faith is about discovering who you are—the remarkable individual God created you to be—because it is out of your *being* that you will do the amazing (and ridiculous) things God has called you to do. God affirms you and, through His Word, your mind is transformed, and your thoughts are aligned with His thoughts. Grace is available for you to walk it out. It takes faith to see beyond the moment you are living in and begin to see yourself as God sees you in the place that He has ordained for you.

> *Grace is available for you to walk it out. It takes faith to see beyond the moment you are living in and begin to see yourself as God sees you in the place that He has ordained for you.*

We see this in the lives of the men and women used by God throughout Scripture. God called them into purpose and destiny, affirmed their identity, and prepared them for the call. Abraham, Isaac, Jacob, Moses, Joshua, Deborah, Gideon, Esther, David, Peter, Paul all had to come to a place of knowing they were who God declared them to be. They had to see beyond the mistakes they may have made, their fears, their lack of training or education. They had to see past the opinions—positive and negative—of others. As we continually say "Yes" and yield to the process, we will see who God created us to be before the foundation of the world was laid.

When my family and I moved back to Cincinnati, I didn't know precisely why God was sending us back. I knew it was to fulfill destiny, and I knew that He was drawing our entire family into a new realm of faith. It wasn't long before He revealed His plan for us, and I entered another season of transitions and changes—a season that required even greater of faith, and a season in which the Lord would reveal who He had created me to be and more of what He'd called me to do.

A New Calling

Not long after moving back to Cincinnati, I reached out to see about the possibility of returning as pastor of Music, Worship and Arts at Christ Emmanuel. But when I realized that wasn't going to work out, I planned to set up offices and continue itinerant ministry through Heirs International Ministries. God soon revealed His plans for me. In mid-July, I traveled to Dallas to the International Worship Institute. There the Lord spoke to my heart: *"When you return home, I want you to start a church."* It wasn't completely surprising to me. My grandfather, Reverend William Thomas Stevenson, had founded Galilee Baptist Church in Columbus. He retired in 1977, and another pastor was set in place. While attending his retirement banquet, the Lord said to me: *"The mantle that was on your grandfather has passed to you."*

I then remembered a conversation I'd had with worship pastor, Judith Christie McAllister. I was still living in Shippensburg and had traveled to Lithonia, Georgia to be a part of a worship conference with Judith and Kirk Franklin at New Birth Missionary Baptist Church at the invitation of Minister Byron Cage.

> **God will often speak to us about the calling on our lives long before He releases us into that calling. We must receive the call, say yes to it, and remain in God's timing.**

"John, when are you going to start your church?" Judith asked as we rode to the church.

"Why would you ask that?"

"It's all over you," she said. "God has called you to be a pastor."

Starting a church wasn't anything I'd considered, but I began to pray about it. And now, a year or so after that conversation, God had spoken. This was the destiny He'd sent us back to Cincinnati to fulfill.

God will often speak to us about the calling on our lives long before He releases us into that calling. We must receive the call, say yes to it, and remain in God's timing. The psalmist David was anointed to be Israel's king years before he ascended to the throne. Even though he knew God had called him to be king, David did not attempt to take the throne ahead of God's timing. We must not be presumptuous and step out ahead of the Lord, nor must we lag behind Him out of uncertainty. Living by faith is hearing Him speak, doing what we know to do, and moving as He directs *when* He directs.

When I returned home from Dallas, I gathered everyone around the dinner table. "God spoke to me. He wants me to start a church," I said. Now I have to tell you, no one was excited about the idea. *No one!* Marissa expressed her concerns, but she said she would follow my lead if that's what God was saying to me. I believed God had called me to pastor, though I wasn't sure how everything would evolve. If we are to walk in the realm of ridiculous faith, while it is natural for us to focus on the "how," we can't let that be our concern. That is God's part.

I started having weekly gatherings in our home with just my family. The Lord had said, "*Start with your wife and five children. Don't invite anyone else to come until I tell you. If your family does not receive you as pastor, I will not release you to pastor anyone else.*" And though I'd had conversations with a handful of individuals who believed they were to be a part of the ministry, I was obedient and begin with just my family. We met every Wednesday evening with a time of worship and time in the Word. After two months or so, others began to meet with us, and as word got out, more families came. Heirs Family Worship Center (now Heirs Covenant Church) was born.

> *To live in a new place of faith and fulfill your assignment, you must be willing to lay down your reputation.*

I'm sure to some who knew me, the idea of me starting a church and stepping into the role of senior pastor was ridiculous. People knew me as a musician and worship leader. Seeing me beyond that was difficult for some. And I had to shift how I saw myself and how I functioned. I had to be willing to set aside any reputation I had, not be concerned with others' opinions of me and see myself as God saw me so I could step courageously and confidently into this new place. I had to grow into it. To live in a new place of faith and fulfill your assignment, you must be willing to lay down your reputation.

I have to admit those early years were some of the most challenging growth experiences of my life. I was not only navigating through the care of my family but the care of other people. I was navigating through working with different personalities and through the intentions of well-meaning people. I knew I was called, but I didn't have the full vision, so others weighed in with *their* vision for the church. And, while I didn't realize it then, I had to work through my own self-imposed limitations.

Grace in Faith

On Sunday, September 21, 1997, at approximately 4:00 P.M. my father laid down to rest and went home to be with the Lord. I was in Detroit, Michigan, ministering to a group of men when he transitioned. It wouldn't be until the following day when I returned home that my wife would sit next to me on the side of the bed and tell me he was gone. I immediately packed a small bag and went to Columbus to help make the arrangements.

The following Friday evening, we held my father's home going service at Galilee Baptist Church, the church founded by his father, my grandfather, Reverend William Thomas Stevenson. I had the honor and wonderful privilege of giving the eulogy. My message was "Pursued by Love, Captured by Grace." My father had run from God's love all his life, but eventually was captured by God's grace. That really is everyone's story! Some just surrender sooner than others. By God's grace, I was able to deliver the message without falling apart.

The next day we buried our dad. After the final words were spoken, my three brothers, my sister and I stood at the graveside, our arms around one another, weeping. It was in that moment, the grace my heavenly Father had given me to walk with my father in his remaining months lifted. I was one of his five children saying a last goodbye to his dad. When we left, I knew I would never go back to that place.

No need to. My father was now in heaven with his father and mother, and they all were with their Father!

My father's transition ended a chapter; a new one was beginning. The journey I would now embark on was one that would forever change my walk with God! My faith in the God with whom all things are possible would grow exponentially as I became the pastor He'd called me to be, and as I faced one of the greatest challenges of my life. I'd learn the reality of Paul's words to the Church in Galatia: to live all of life, not just by faith *in* the Son, but by the faith *of* Jesus Christ (Galatians 2:20 KJV). These next years would stretch me, reveal what was in me, test and challenge me, and teach me and my family to walk in levels of faith we'd not known before.

Chapter 9

Confidently, Consistently, Courageously

> *Consider it all joy, my brethren, when you encounter various trials, knowing that the testing of your faith produces endurance. And let endurance have its perfect result, so that you may be perfect and complete, lacking in nothing.*
>
> James 1:2-4

These words from the first chapter of James' epistle may be some of the most challenging words in the Bible. The J.B. Philips Translation reads this way: **When all kinds of trials and temptations crowd into your lives my brothers, don't resent them as intruders, but welcome them as friends!** It is natural for us to resist and fight against anything that appears to have the potential to harm us, make things difficult for us, or even try to take us out. And yet James tells us to count those things as joy, to make them our friends. We can welcome them as friends when we understand what trials, challenges, pressure, and even pain are designed to produce in us. While the enemy of our souls is after our faith, God uses trials to produce endurance. That word in the Greek means to stand or abide under the pressure without surrendering to it. It requires us to submit to the process instead of fighting against it, and that is only possible when we can see beyond the test. James tells us that on the other side of the trial—if we endure—is the fulfillment of purpose, maturity, wholeness, completion. We emerge lacking nothing!

Jesus Christ is our perfect example. We read in Hebrews 12 that Christ endured the cross because of the joy He saw beyond it. That joy was you and me, reconciled to the Father, free from sin, healed and whole, adopted into the family, heirs of God, and joint heirs with Christ. He saw the triumph of the cross and, therefore, was able to endure it all.

> *Therefore, since we have so great a cloud of witnesses surrounding us, let us also lay aside every encumbrance and the sin which so easily entangles us, and let us run with endurance the race that is set before us, fixing our eyes on Jesus, the author and perfecter of faith, who for the joy set before Him endured the cross, despising the shame, and has sat down at the right hand of the throne of God. For consider Him who has endured such hostility by sinners against Himself, so that you will not grow weary and lose heart (Hebrews 12:1-3).*

The Bible does not promise a life free of challenges. It lets us know that we can expect them. You need to know that the moment you choose to live this life of faith, your choice will be tested, and along with the test will come options and ways out. In those times of testing, you must know what God is speaking specifically to you. The Word of God declares that we are triumphant when we choose to stand on His promises without wavering. We will not be disappointed. Living in the realm of ridiculous faith is living in a place of trust in God in challenging times, under pressure, in tests and in trials. Yes, those times certainly will come, but God uses them for our making. Choose to stand firm on the promise that He works it all for good (Romans 8:28). He knows the way we take, and when we have been tried (proved), we shall come forth as gold (Job 23:11).

A New Season, A Different Realm

1997 was a pivotal year in my life: our family moved, we began the church, and my father went home to be with the Lord. I had entered a season of proving and being perfected in ways I could never have imagined. I hadn't expected the early years of growing a church to be necessarily easy, but I trusted God to send the right people to help build Heirs Family Worship Center into the church He'd ordained it to be. The Lord did send many gifted, talented, and committed individuals. I'd believed that God was calling us to build a place for those who had grown weary with religion, who were hungry for the manifest Presence of God, who desired to discover and fulfill purpose, and who wanted to see the power of God in demonstration. And that is who He sent. I hadn't realized all the Lord desired to do in me that would not only prepare me to pastor with His heart, but also prepare me to step confidently into the authority He'd given me. He was freeing me to live in a new realm of faith and to learn to trust in Him at all costs. The church grew, and soon we had to move our services from our home.

On Resurrection Sunday, 1998, we held our first service in the Heritage Elementary School cafetorium. Each Sunday we'd have to set up and then break down all the equipment from chairs to the sound system. God continued to bless us with His Presence, and as more families came, it soon became apparent that we needed a place of our own. We found a space to lease in a shopping plaza that had been a David's Bridal. Our leadership team sat in that space one day, imagining the possibilities and casting vision. That space became the new home of Heirs Family Worship Center.

We had plans drawn up and began transforming the roughly 10,000 square feet. We held our first service on New Year's Eve of 1999 while construction continued.

I was learning to step into this new place that God had for me and learning to walk in a level of confidence I'd not had before. Some of that learning was painful. God has a way of helping us see ourselves and areas in us that need growth and transformation. We had invested a sizable amount of money in building out the space we were leasing. Soon after the build-out was complete, we hit a financial wall, and it became difficult to honor our financial obligations. The Board asked me to take a cut in salary. I was willing to make that sacrifice, but for the wrong reason. And that decision proved to be very difficult for me and my family. We suffered financially over the next two years.

During that time, I cried out to God, seeking answers. I decided to fast and pray. While on the fast, God spoke to me: "*I did not require you to spend as much as you did to build out the space.*" Then He said, "*When you took the pay cut, you did it out of fear and not faith; you feared that they would leave you.*" I shared with my wife what the Lord had said to me. We prayed, and I repented!

Shortly after that, I met with our board members. I held nothing against them. They were just trying to help make sound decisions for the sake of the ministry. I told them what the Lord had revealed to me. It was painful for me to admit it, but it was true. My confidence and security had not been rooted in God alone. I had suffered needlessly because I hadn't kept my eyes on Him. I had repented—changed my thinking—and I was not going to live in that place of fear any longer. It was not about those who'd asked me to take the pay cut; it was about me and my desire that God be first in my life and that I please Him above all else. Through God's grace and mercy, I was able to change and grow. As a result of that experience, I learned my trust must be solely in God.

Know Who You Are

Those early years of the ministry were my initiation, and it often felt like initiation by fire. It took years for me to grow confident in who God had called me to be, and in my ability to hear His voice and to stand resolute in what I heard. God had called me to pastor His people, and He was transforming me through brokenness into the pastor He knew I could be. It took about seven years for me to make the shift I needed to make. And as I did, some people chose to leave the ministry. But I had settled in a place of faith that allowed me to be OK with that. I have had to learn that no matter who comes or who goes, no matter how gifted or skilled they are, no matter how educated or financially successful they are, my focus has to remain on the Lord, what He has spoken to me and the vision that He has given me. He is the one who has called me, and

> *Living in the realm of ridiculous faith is not just exercising faith to receive things. It is faith to be who God created you to be and do what He called you to do.*

He will be the one to keep me and keep His church. He provides all that is needed.

Living in the realm of ridiculous faith is not just exercising faith to receive things. It is faith to *be* who God created you to be and do what He called you to do. You will not be able to fulfill the call on your life and complete your assignment until you are confident in who you are. You cannot need the affirmation of others. Nor can you continually make yourself small to accommodate others and expect to be effective in the place God has set you. It may take you some time to shed old mindsets and make that shift to stand boldly in your calling. And you can be sure there will be those who will not like it when you do. They may misinterpret your actions and words; they may see your new-found confidence as arrogance; they may attempt to malign you or discredit you; they may walk away.

> *You will not be able to fulfill the call on your life and complete your assignment until you are confident in who you are.*

I know that can be hurtful and disheartening. But you must recognize their actions most often reflect something in them that needs to be healed—something only God can heal. When you desire to please the Father rather than man and allow Him full access to your heart, He will reveal anything in you that is not like Him, any area that needs to be healed, anything that requires repentance. God will release the grace to make any adjustments and changes you need to make. Receive that grace, then see Him do what only He can.

Affirmed by the Father

When Jesus began His ministry, hordes of people followed Him. They were drawn by the miracles and the authority with which He spoke. He fed them and showed compassion towards them. But as He preached His message and as He declared His identity and purpose, they became challenged. Some could only see Him as Joseph's son. Still, others misunderstood the purpose of His coming. He wasn't the "savior" they anticipated. They wanted Him to set up an earthly kingdom and even tried to force His hand. Others just followed Him because of the miracles. Had Jesus not been confident in who He was and why He'd come, had He felt a need to please everyone to receive their support, had He feared people walking away, He could not have accomplished what He came to do.

But Jesus had heard His Father's voice on the day of His baptism in the Jordan River. ***"This is My beloved Son, in whom I am well-pleased."*** Those words from the Father settled everything. Regardless of what others thought or said about Him, whether they stayed or walked away, whether they understood His mission and method or not, whether they believed He was the Son of God or not, He remained resolute. He didn't seek the affirmation of others; He'd been affirmed by His Father, and that was more than enough.

> ***God wants you to walk confidently in who He has called you to be. He wants you to confidently walk out your faith. He wants you to confidently walk out your purpose and fulfill your destiny.***

God wants you to walk confidently in who He has called you to be. He wants you to confidently walk out your faith. He wants you to confidently walk out your purpose and fulfill your destiny. Can you believe He is saying to you the exact words He spoke to Jesus? *You* are His beloved, in whom He is well-pleased. He is the one who defines you. It is accepting this truth that will empower you. Let His words of affirmation ring louder than what others think of you, say about you, may even do to impede your progress or move you out of your assignment. You can be confident that the same God who called you, the same God who began a good work in you, is the same God completing that work in you (Philippians 1:6), and He is using everything and everyone in your life as part of the process.

God used those early years of Heirs Family Worship Center to move me to another place of faith and reliance on Him, but the church was not the only thing drawing me more deeply into that realm of ridiculous faith.

"We really need to do something about this," Dr. Cox, my primary care physician, said. A routine physical examination in 1997 revealed that I had an elevated PSA (Prostate-Specific Antigens). The normal range is 0-4; mine was 4.8. An elevated PSA may indicate any number of conditions. My doctor, who is a believer, was careful not to say it may be cancer. He only said we'd need to keep an eye on it. I shared the results with Marissa and told her my posture was to watch it and pray. The following year, I had another physical exam, and now the number was 7, warranting a visit with a urologist.

"We just need to remove your prostate, so you don't have to concern yourself about it," the urologist said. I was 40 years old, and the idea of surgery of this kind—just to be safe—did not set well with me. I understand doctors are trained to look at the numbers and often recommend a treatment plan based on the statistical outcomes. But something in me was not willing to accept what he was saying.

"That's absolutely not going to happen," I announced.

"I hope your life insurance is paid up," he shot back.

He was trying to frighten me into surgery, and I knew that was not God. At that moment, I made a choice: I would stand on the Word of God and allow Him to show me how He wanted to bring about my healing. I just believed that the traditional approach, with all its side effects, was not for me. Jesus had secured my healing on the cross, and I would wait to see how that healing would manifest.

I did not see that urologist again.

I didn't realize it at the time, but God had issued me another invitation to live in the realm of ridiculous faith, a greater opportunity to deepen my relationship with Him and to strengthen my faith in Him as I began a 15-year journey that would forever change me.

Chapter 10

What Are You Requiring of Me?

Yet he did not waver through unbelief regarding the promise of God, but was strengthened in his faith and gave glory to God, being fully persuaded that God had power to do what he had promised.
Romans 4:20,21 NKJV

"Whatever I do must be out of faith, not out of fear," I told my primary care physician. "And when I hear from God, I'll know exactly what to do."

By 2009, my PSA had risen to 11. I know my decision to wait until I heard from the Lord challenged my doctor. He watched as the numbers continued to rise and, from a medical perspective, waiting was not a luxury he believed I had. I knew my trust in God and His Word had to be stronger than fear of the numbers. I knew I had a covenantal right to healing and wholeness. I just didn't know the "how," and until I did, I would wait.

Waiting is not something most of us enjoy. We live in a time where so much is quickly accessible and attainable; we want what we want when we want it. We often exercise our faith, hoping that which we are believing for will quickly manifest in our lives. We often fail to recognize that God is moving in the wait, and we must be careful not to allow impatience, our desire for a quick fix, fear, or just our need for certainty to cause us to miss what God is doing in us, and sometimes in others, through the waiting process. We don't want to forfeit the greater glory God desires to receive because we grew uncomfortable in the wait.

Trust me, I know waiting is not always easy. It's during those times of uncertainty that our emotions try to get the better of us. Feelings of fear, anxiousness, confusion may come and try to force us into making quick decisions or listening to voices other than God's. We must learn to wait on Him despite what we feel. The Father is teaching us to trust Him, even when it seems nothing is happening. He wants us to trust Him when nothing seems to change, when, in fact, things seem to be getting worse. It takes just as much faith to wait as it does to step out in what we believe the Lord is speaking. But there is always grace in the wait.

> *It takes just as much faith to wait as it does to step out in what we believe the Lord is speaking. But there is always grace in the wait.*

Abraham knew something about waiting. We read in Romans 4 that he did not become "weak in faith" as he waited for the promise of an heir to be fulfilled.

> **He did not weaken in faith when he considered his own body as [already] dead (for he was almost a hundred years old) and the dead womb of Sarah. He did not doubt God's promise in unbelief; rather, he was empowered by faith and gave glory to God and was fully convinced that what he had promised he was also able to do (Romans 4:19-21 NABRE).**

Abraham was not ignorant of the facts. He was fully aware that, in the natural, he and Sarah were incapable of producing a child. And yet, he did not allow the facts to override the promise of God. *The Passion Translation* says Abraham did not allow his faith to be "undermined" by the facts. He made a choice and would not allow the circumstances to move him. And even though he did not always walk out his faith perfectly, he never gave up on the promise. He is an example of those who received the promise because they patiently waited (Hebrews 6:15). Living in the realm of ridiculous faith will often mean waiting. But there are some things you and I can do in the process that help us maintain a firm faith and posture us to receive grace in the wait.

A Heart of Repentance

I have always endeavored to live in a place of brokenness before the Lord. I want to be able to hear Him; I want to respond in obedience to whatever He speaks. When things are not lining up the way I believe they should, I search within. I know, if there is a problem, it's not with God. I asked Him to reveal anything I may have said or done that may have been a gateway to what is going on in my life or may be the cause of any delay. I've learned to pray a prayer we all must be willing to pray, "Lord, show me me!"

So much was happening in my life in addition to the health challenge. After a season of significant growth at Heirs, the numbers began to dwindle. Several people left, some offended, and I started wondering if I'd lost my effectiveness. I was praying about how to move the ministry forward. I asked God to show me anything in my past I needed to address that could be affecting my continued growth or the growth of the ministry.

"When you left Rhema, you didn't leave in the right way," I heard the Lord say.

I'd left Rhema Christian Center in 1989 offended, and now I was seeing others leave Heirs the same way. I recognize that some things from our past, when left unresolved, have a way of showing up again. The Lord was helping me make the connection.

I immediately called Rhema and asked to meet with Apostle Scales, only to be told that his schedule was full and would not open up for weeks out. That wasn't going to work for me. I knew I needed to repent and make things right with Lafayette and the others I'd felt had wronged me as soon as I could.

> **Some things from our past, when left unresolved, have a way of showing up again.**

So nearly 15 years after leaving Rhema, I, along with some of the brothers from Heirs, drove to Columbus to a men's conference the church was having. The conference was secondary for me; my intention was to see Apostle Scales. God orchestrated that meeting.

"When I left here, I didn't leave in the right way," I said to him. "I need to ask your forgiveness."

He was very gracious. He said there was no need to apologize. It had been a long time ago, and our relationship was good. But I knew what the Lord had told me. This was something I needed to do. I then found Lafayette's administrator, Bill Dotson, and Dennis Wade, one of the elders, and I apologized to them as well. They, too, told me it wasn't necessary. But I knew this act of repentance was a turning point for me in my relationship with them and, most importantly, in my relationship with the Lord. I also believe that moment of repentance and reconciliation closed what could have been a revolving door of offense.

While things had been made right with those that I felt had wronged me, I knew there were members of the congregation who had taken on my offense out of their love for me and were still carrying it. I knew I had to do something that would help free them. And that opportunity came when Rhema invited my spiritual son, Darwin Hobbs, to give a concert, and they asked me to introduce him.

When I got up, I heard the Holy Spirit say, *"Now you need to repent publicly."* Standing before a sanctuary packed with worshipers, I asked Darwin's permission to share something. I then addressed those who had been at Rhema when I served as the worship leader.

"When I left Rhema, I left offended. I left hurt. What many of you do not know is that since that time, I have repented and reconciled my relationship with Lafayette Scales, Bill Dotson, and Dennis Wade. I feel led by God to share this with you so you can be OK with it." That settled it and closed that door.

I sought God for any open doors that may have been an inroad to what I was dealing with physically. I wanted to know if there was anger, unforgiveness, resentment, offense, hurt, bitterness—anything! In seasons of waiting, we must ask the Lord to show us anything in our lives that could be problematic without fearing what He may reveal.

> *In seasons of waiting, we must ask the Lord to show us anything in our lives that could be problematic without fearing what He may reveal.*

We must be intentional about finding anything we've done, are presently doing, or have not dealt with that may be allowing things to manifest in our lives or may present future problems if not addressed.

When He shows us, we must be willing to repent and do whatever He instructs us to do to make things right. Repentance is an act of faith and frees us of every possible hindrance to the fulfillment of God's promises.

Speak Life

From the moment I'd received news of my elevated PSA, I was mindful of what I spoke. Now 12 years into the journey, I became even more intentional as I waited to hear from the Lord. It was during this time that I really learned the power of speaking faith-filled words. When you and I are waiting to get clear direction, we must learn to monitor what we say and what we allow others to say to us. Proverbs 18:21 tells us death and life are in the power of the tongue. I like how the Message says it: "***Words kill, words give life; they're either poison or fruit—you choose.***" When we are not mindful of the words we speak, we can give life to things that we shouldn't. We have a choice. To maintain a firm faith when facing challenges of any kind, we must purposefully align our words with God's Word and, if necessary, help others in our world to do the same.

> *To maintain a firm faith when facing challenges of any kind, we must purposefully align our words with God's Word and, if necessary, help others in our world to do the same.*

If we truly believe the Word of God, then we speak it in faith. I was careful never to say, "I have. . ." I refused to take ownership of something Jesus bore on the cross for me. To some, it may have seemed I was in denial of the diagnosis. I wasn't. I was well aware of what the doctors were saying, and when I did speak of it, I'd say, "The doctors say…" or "The diagnosis is…" But I would not allow my words to give life to it, nor would I permit it to operate in my body by what I spoke.

I was also mindful with whom I shared any information. Initially, only Marissa knew. Words—ours and those of others—create constructs. Well-meaning people can say things, not knowing that they are adding to the problem rather than encouraging you. I did not want to share what I was walking through and have others create their scenarios or weigh in on what I should do. Some I knew would respond out of emotion, and I didn't want people pulling me into their emotional space. Neither did I want them speaking anything into the atmosphere that was shrouded in fear. I chose to share it with individuals who I knew I could trust to pray.

If you are to live in the realm of ridiculous faith—especially during seasons of waiting—it is essential that you surround yourself with people who will speak faith-filled words and pray in line with Scripture. It doesn't matter if you're facing a challenge with health, finances, relationships, or navigating through walking out purpose. You must not only be mindful of how you speak about your circumstances but what you will allow others to say. If necessary, negate their words with the truth of God's Word. At one point in the journey, I felt directed by Holy Spirit to share, via email, with a few individuals. One brother wrote back, "John, I'm delighted to know your cancer is contained."

I was quick to respond, "It's not *my* cancer. Jesus bore it on the cross; it doesn't belong to me." And he quickly responded to me, "I'm sorry! You are so right."

You can't be hesitant in correcting people, even at the risk of offending them. You must learn to see every challenge or test in light of the finished work of Christ, speak from that position and help others shift the way they see and talk about it.

I don't mean to suggest that it's easy. It wasn't *easy* for me. I'd often find myself counseling other men who were walking through the same health challenge. I had to be intentional, as I listened to them, not to take on their fear or allow their decisions to move me. I chose to speak the Word of God to them, not just to encourage them but also to feed my faith. I was careful not to tell them what to do. They would need to hear from the Lord for themselves. I have learned in this walk of faith that each person's path is different, and the way God may be leading me is not necessarily the way for someone else. I was intentional about listening to teachings and scriptures on healing. I reached out to Word of Faith ministries, such as Kenneth Copeland and Bill Winston, for teachings that fed and strengthened my faith while I encouraged others in theirs.

Find the Place of Worship

In 2010, I agreed to have a biopsy. "We've found cancer in your prostate," the doctors told me when the results came back. At that time, the doctor gave me the same options that everyone with this diagnosis receives.

"None of those work for me," I told him, and I continued to seek God.

I had learned to pray a simple prayer during those years: "Father, what are You requiring of me in light of what I now know?" You see, sometimes we, unintentionally, pray as if we are informing God of something He doesn't already know. Or we pray, asking Him to do something He has already done. When we receive information, it isn't news to God, nor is it something He has to work out. We simply need to know our next step, if there is a next step to take.

> *"Father, what are You requiring of me in light of what I now know?"*

New information may be the piece we need to move forward, but I am also aware that new information often can devastate us, shake our faith, cause us to question ourselves and question God. That is when we find a place of worship that enables us to find peace and rest in Him. Then we can process any information that comes to us in the light of His Presence. Life in the realm of ridiculous faith requires a disciplined worship life.

Worship has been one of the primary things that has kept me focused when facing challenges or in seasons of waiting. It is through worship that I have a greater awareness of His presence and I hear Him speak. I am fortunate to play and write songs, and every time I need to find strength and resolve, I write. Every song I have written has resulted from where I found myself and became a song that brought peace and fortitude to me long before others hear it. But worship is not just about singing or playing an instrument. True worship is beyond the music. You and I were created as worshipers—those who are intimately acquainted with and who have a daily relationship with God exhibited through obedience. Sometimes that simply means getting still and waiting in His presence. Waiting is as much a part of worship as any musical or verbal expression.

David understood the importance of worship when needing to hear from the Lord. We see that throughout his life, but it is clearly demonstrated in 1 Samuel 30. David and his men return to Ziklag from battle to discover that the Amalekites had attacked Ziklag, burned it, and captured the women and children. In their mourning, the men blamed David and wanted to stone him. Then we read:

And David was greatly distressed; for the people spake of stoning him, because the soul of all the people was grieved, every man for his sons and for his daughters: but David encouraged himself in the Lord his God (1 Samuel 30:6 KJV).

David did what he always did; he found a place of worship and "strengthened himself in the Lord." He found that place in the Presence of God, the only place of absolute peace and strength. From that posture of worship, he gained insight, strength, wisdom, and direction. I believe that after David found that place of worship, focused and attuned to the Lord, he was able to do what we all must do when we find ourselves in challenging situations. From that place of worship, David was able to:

- *Assess the situation.*
- *Accept the challenge that the situation presented.*
- *Access the power of the Kingdom in faith through prayer, praise, worship, declaration and proclamation of the Word of God.*
- *Actively engage by exercising Kingdom authority.*

Then he was able to ask, "Shall I pursue this troop?" But he could only find his way to ask and receive clear direction from a place of worship. It was in the place of worship that David heard God speak, *"Pursue, for you shall surely overtake them and without fail recover all"* (1 Sam. 30:8).

When you find yourself in challenging times, you must posture yourself as David did. Get away and find a place of worship. In the Presence of the Lord you find the peace that enables you to see from God's perspective and hear His voice clearly.

> **In challenging times, find a place of worship. In the Presence of the Lord you find the peace that enables you to see from God's perspective and hear His voice clearly.**

Remain Consistent in the Wait

While waiting on God, you and I must remain consistent in our faith and our actions. Romans 4 tells us the Abraham did not waver in his faith. He remained consistent. I believe a Holy Spirit strategy for me was to focus on God by continuing to do what I was doing with the church and in ministry as a whole. I was conscious of the challenge, but I wouldn't allow myself to be preoccupied with it. When you are waiting on the Lord, don't be passive. Continue to do what you know to do. Continue to walk out purpose as God has revealed it to you. Continue to confess the Word, declare His promises and keep your focus on Him.

I continued traveling, making several trips to South Africa with my pastor, Bishop Joseph Garlington, and his Reconciliation team. I also traveled to England, Singapore, and Ethiopia to minister. I worked closely with my dear friend and brother, Ford Taylor, to co-found Transformation Cincinnati/Northern Kentucky and worked with other city leaders to see transformation in our city. I recorded the *Hear My Heart* CD and published my third book, *Worshiper by Design: A Unique Look at Why We were Created*.

> *The consistency of faith will ultimately produce progressive growth that will lead to new levels, dimensions, and realms of faith that will allow us to access the seemingly unimaginable, the unbelievable, to apprehend the seemingly unattainable!*

You and I are to remain consistent in our faith, not only by the confession we make but by the life we live as we wait. I believe that is how the Lord gets the glory from our lives. The Apostle Paul tells us that Abraham grew strong in faith and "gave glory to God." The Greek word for glory is "doxa," and it means "that which gives a proper opinion" or "reputation." Everything Abraham said and did gave a "proper opinion" of God. All his actions declared who he knew God to be.

That consistency of faith is what distinguishes those who live in the realm of ridiculous faith from others. Remaining consistent in our attitude, in our words, and in our actions is the way we acknowledge God's power, His greatness, His faithfulness, and His wisdom.

The consistency of faith will ultimately produce progressive growth that will lead to new levels, dimensions, and realms of faith that will allow us to access the seemingly unimaginable, the unbelievable, to apprehend the seemingly unattainable!

Chapter 11

The Process of Perfect Timing

And so, having patiently waited, he obtained the promise.
Hebrews 6:15

Twenty-five years is a long time to hold onto a promise. As Abraham grew older and older, the likelihood of fathering a child—at least in the natural—grew less and less. And yet, the Bible tells us that he "patiently endured"—at age 80, 85, 90, 95, 99. His conviction that God was more than able to do what He'd promised remained strong. Abraham understood covenant. Even when made between human beings, it was a serious and unbreakable commitment. How much more would the God of the universe, the God who spoke the world into existence, the covenant-making God honor His word? We read in Hebrews 6 that because there was no one greater to swear by, God swore by Himself.

> *Now when God made a promise to Abraham, since there was no one greater than himself, he swore an oath on his own integrity to keep the promise as sure as God exists! So he said, "Have no doubt, I promise to bless you over and over, and give you a son and multiply you without measure!* (Hebrews 6:13-14 The Passion Translation)

During those years of waiting, Abraham learned the nature and character of the One who had promised. He learned what truly constitutes a firm faith. He grew to know what all those who desire to live in the realm of ridiculous faith must learn. He realized that we must maintain:

- *A firm conviction that God is able to do what He says He will do.*
- *A firm confession that speaks the desired outcome.*
- *A firm commitment to pursue at all costs—at any cost.*
- *A firm consistency in actions and attitude.*
- *A firm courageous spirit that overcomes fear and defies logic.*

Abraham stood firmly on what he knew and trusted God with that which he did not understand.

If you have been walking with God for any length of time, I'm sure you realize that He is not on your schedule. He will often allow things to play out in such a way that only He can turn them around. He allows them to go in a way that makes it impossible for us to rely on our strength or wisdom. He moves in ways that allow Him, and only Him, to get the glory! And He does it in such a way that enables others to know He is the faithful One, the one and only God.

> *God doesn't let us in on every detail; He reveals just enough information to move us from point A to point B or to encourage us as we wait. That's the nature of life in the realm of ridiculous faith.*

God doesn't let us in on every detail; He reveals just enough information to move us from point A to point B or to encourage us as we wait. That's the nature of life in the realm of ridiculous faith. God teaches us to walk by faith and not by sight. The Lord wants us to grow to trust Him in deeper, fuller ways. He is working all things together for our good in such a magnificent way so He receives the maximum glory from our lives.

Wait, Wait, Wait

It would be another two years before I'd know what action I was to take. In the meantime, I was doing all I knew to do, both naturally and spiritually. My pastors, Bishop Joseph and Pastor Barbara Garlington, put me in contact with their doctor in Jeannette, Pennsylvania. He dealt with holistic medicine, and after a thorough workup, he prescribed a regimen of supplements that I faithfully took. I upped my exercise routine and maintained a healthy diet. As I continued to seek the Lord for His direction, I shared what was going on with a few more individuals. I told our five children and one of my personal intercessors. I knew I needed the prayer covering from those I trusted to pray confidentially and who I knew could hear from the Lord.

In July of 2012, I had another physical. This time the PSA was 15, which greatly alarmed my physician. He was concerned that any cancer that may have been in my body had now spread, and I was in trouble. So he scheduled me for a full-body bone scan and a pelvic CT scan. Thanks be to God! Nothing had spread! But I knew it was time to take action, though I still hadn't heard from the Lord what steps to take. Marissa was very concerned, and I'm sure she thought I was in denial. But I had chosen to take the same posture that the prophet Micah writes of:

But as for me, I will watch expectantly for the Lord;
I will wait for the God of my salvation.
My God will hear me (Micah 7:7).

God knew better than anyone what was going in the body He had created, and I believed He'd reveal His plan for me at the right time. I'd continue to patiently wait and combat any thoughts that did not align with the Word of God and with the covenant I have with Him through Jesus Christ. I admit that when my PSA reached 15, I had to press even more into a place of faith to overcome any feelings of fear or anxiety. My doctor's concern was now being projected onto me. Just before having the CT, I was injected with iodine. I'd gone to First Watch, one of my favorite breakfast spots, and I found myself continually combatting concerns about what the test might reveal.

You and I will find spiritual warfare is necessary to remain steadfast in our faith, and we will have to do what the Apostle Paul tells us: "...***casting down arguments and every high thing that exalts itself against the knowledge of God, bringing every thought into captivity to the obedience of Chris***t..." (2 Corinthians 10:5).

In August, I received an email from a dear friend, one of the intercessors I'd had praying for me. The email contained a vlog post from a gentleman in Atlanta, Georgia, named Boyd Bailey. She had been receiving his daily devotions, "Wisdom Hunters," and was about to delete this particular one until she noticed that it was a video update on his health. After watching it, she forwarded it to me.

Boyd had been diagnosed with prostate cancer. Through his urologist, he was introduced to a procedure called High-Intensity Focused Ultrasound (HIFU). In his vlog, he shared how the Lord had led him to have that procedure, and now he was completely healed. No cancer in his body! He added that anyone interested in more information about HIFU could reach out to him. I shared the video with Marissa, and she encouraged me to contact him. I emailed him that day.

The next day Boyd called me. We talked a bit about the procedure. He'd had to go to Montreal, Canada to have it done. HIFU was still in the clinical trial phase in the US and was not FDA-approved.

"If you're interested," Boyd said, "I can give you the name of my urologist. He has dual citizenship in the US and Canada and could do the procedure in Canada if you're a candidate."

I contacted the urologist and had the urologist I was seeing send my medical records to his office in Atlanta. Then Marissa and I made a trip to meet with him.

"I believe you are an excellent candidate for HIFU," he said after examining me.

The next day Marissa and I met with Boyd and his wife in their home. He shared his story with us, and we prayed together. It was in that moment, sitting in the Bailey home, sipping iced tea, I knew what I was to do.

"I believe this is what the Lord wants me to do," I told Marissa on the drive home. She expressed her concerns because it was not FDA-approved, but she continued to pray with me that the Lord would confirm we were heading in the right direction.

When I got home, I called Bishop Garlington and told him what I believe God was speaking to me. I also shared with him what I needed to make it happen. The cost of the procedure, which was not covered by insurance, was $25.000. I'd need an additional $5,000 to cover all other expenses, airfare and a hotel room for a couple of days while I rested and recuperated in Canada.

"We'll believe with you for that," Bishop said.

And by faith, I scheduled the procedure for November.

The Favor Factor

The Bible is filled with examples of individuals who exercised faith and found great favor. Anyone used by God experienced His favor. Joseph, Moses, David, Esther, Paul, and even Jesus Himself accomplished great things, yes, by faith, and because God's favor was evident in their lives. David wrote, **For You bless the righteous person, Lord, You surround him with favor as with a shield.** (Psalm 5:12).

You and I are righteous, made so through Jesus' work on the cross. Therefore, we can be sure that the favor of God surrounds *us* like a shield. Favor is ours because of the covenant we have with the Lord. It, like grace, mercy, love, salvation, is not something we earn. God gives it! And it's not just given to a select few; *all believers receive it.* All just don't recognize it. All don't walk in it or exercise it.

> *Favor is ours because of the covenant we have with the Lord. It, like grace, mercy, love, salvation, is not something we earn. God gives it!*

The favor of the Lord has been on my life all my life, even when I didn't realize it or steward it well. I define favor as unmerited kindness and goodness shown to one through various gestures, gifts, and acts evidenced in uncommon promotions, advantages, opportunities, prosperity, resources, and increase. I've seen it demonstrated in my life in something as simple as a store clerk not charging me for my daily cup of coffee to total strangers paying for my dry cleaning to the grand gesture of being gifted automobiles. I'm grateful for it all.

> *The same God who provided for you in the past, the same God who delivered you in the past, the same God who healed you in the past is the same God who will provide, deliver, heal now!*

God had just invited me to step even further into the realm of ridiculous faith. He'd revealed the means through which my healing would come, and now I needed to trust Him for the funds. I didn't have $30,000 for the procedure. But I did have a history with God. I'd seen Him move to provide just what I needed, just when I needed it. Once you have seen God move in your life in one situation, it's not difficult to trust Him in your current situation, no matter how complex it may seem. The same God who provided for you in the past, the same God who delivered you in the past, the same God who healed you in the past is the same God who will provide, deliver, heal now! As you and I grow in our awareness of the Kingdom of God, we realize that everything we need is available to us in His Kingdom. It doesn't matter how ridiculous it seems. God has not changed, and nothing is too hard (or ridiculous) for Him.

This is a reality for all who choose to walk in a greater place of faith: faith and favor go hand-in-hand. You and I do have the responsibility of recognizing it and stewarding it. The challenge may be that favor is not readily seen until you're in the moment. But when you are aware, you learn to exercise it. You learn the power of "The Ask."

By faith, I knew that every cent I needed for the procedure would come. I didn't know how, but the 'how' is always God's business. Our responsibility is to act in obedience when He directs us. As we survey Scripture, we see an "ask" is often involved. When the Lord sent Moses back to Egypt to deliver Israel from bondage, He told Moses: ***"And I will give this people favor in the sight of the Egyptians; and it shall be, when you go, that you shall not go empty-handed"*** (Exodus 3:21).

We later read:
> ***Now the children of Israel had done according to the word of Moses, and they had asked from the Egyptians articles of silver, articles of gold, and clothing. And the Lord had given the people favor in the sight of the Egyptians, so that they granted them what they requested. Thus they plundered the Egyptians*** (Exodus 12:35-36 emphasis added).

They *asked* and saw the favor of the Lord! And it's in the power of "The Ask" that we often see God's favor unfold in our lives.

After I'd scheduled the procedure, the Lord directed me to compose a letter to send to 15 specific individuals. The letter traced the journey of my trusting God, believing Him, and waiting on Him to show me how He wanted to bring healing. I shared what the doctors had said, and I believed that HIFU was the direction I was to take. I also told them about Boyd Bailey and how the Lord had connected us. Then

I shared the procedure's cost and asked them to prayerfully consider sowing whatever the Lord laid on their hearts. I emailed it to those the Lord had shown me.

Once I was clear on the direction, I shared first with my pastors and leadership team and then with our congregation. They'd known nothing about what I'd been walking through over those 15 years. I shared with them what I'd believed the Lord for all those years and what I now knew I needed to do. I shared with them the door that God had opened for me.

In October, Heirs Covenant Church celebrated our 15th anniversary with special services and a formal banquet. Bishop Garlington came from Pittsburgh and brought several checks with him. He also encouraged our body to give. I am grateful to God for His favor and the way He moved on the hearts of individuals. Everyone I'd emailed responded generously. Within 30 days, the Lord blessed me with forty-seven thousand dollars, and I was able to pay for the procedure in cash.

Faith on Foreign Soil

It was a frigid November in Montreal, Canada, when my wife, our daughter, Leslie, and I arrived. It was the last Thursday in November of 2012. Just a week earlier, on Thanksgiving Day, I had told my mother and my siblings what had been going on with me and the procedure I was going to have. And now I was checking into a hotel in a foreign country, knowing the following day would end my 15-year odyssey.

The previous Sunday, I'd stood before our congregation. "I only need you to pray two things," I told them. "Pray *Successful procedure; miraculous recovery.*" (And we still pray that prayer for anyone facing surgery of any kind).

The entire trip seemed surreal to me—almost "otherworldly" in a sense. I knew God had brought me here, but it was all so unfamiliar. I was blessed to not only have Marissa with me but my daughter as well. Leslie has a way of processing things that made her presence necessary. We'd met with the nurse who walked us through the procedure and outlined all the medication I'd need to take and when I'd need to take it. Unknown to me, Leslie took notes and created a detailed calendar for me, which was an absolute blessing. A woman of strong faith, she and her mother kept me covered in prayer along with my family, friends, and congregation in the States.

The next morning, we rose, dressed, and met the nurse in the hotel's lobby, and together, we walked in the bitter, biting cold to the facility, which was only a block from the hotel. The night before, I'd listened over and over to the recording, *I Still Win: A Declaration of Victory and Triumph*. I needed to keep my mind from wandering. I knew the Word of God would still my mind and build my faith.

"Are you ready?" the doctor asked when he came in.

"Yeah, I'm ready!" I wasn't in the least bit tentative, and he knew I was ready to end this journey once and for all. He again went over the procedure, which could take from 3-5 hours, and they began prepping me. In less than three hours, I woke up in recovery. My wife had been communicating my progress with one of our pastors, who in turn, shared updates with the congregation. It had been a successful procedure! All was well! I had gone to Montreal with a PSA of 18. Three months later, the first reading was less than 0, and to this day, I am completely healed!

That evening following the procedure, I was resting in our hotel room, reclining in a chair, feet propped on an ottoman, and I began to reflect on the incredible journey that had led to that moment. I'd never imagined myself making a trip to a foreign country, a country I'd never had a desire to visit, for a procedure that had not been approved in my own country. And yet, this had been the path the Lord had carved out for me to not only bring physical healing, but to teach me lessons I may never have learned taking another route. These words in the book of Job came to mind: **"But He knows the way I take; When He has tried me, I shall come forth as gold** (Job 23:10).

He knew the path, but I didn't, and over those fifteen years, I often felt lost. All along the way, I would hear God speak to me:

Wait!

Rest!

Be patient!

All along the way, He'd tell me who to speak with, who not speak with; who to listen to, who not to listen to; what to read, what not to read. And I realized that there are times for all of us when we feel lost on our faith journey. I thought about the GPS in automobiles. I remember how apprehensive I was initially about using the GPS; it was all so new to me. I'd put in the coordinates, and I had to rely on that voice to get to my destination. I remember my first trip in the first car I owned with GPS. The whole time I kept wondering, "Is this leading me in the right direction?" Ultimately, it got me where I was going, and over time, I learned to trust the system; I learned to trust the voice. But it had been a learning process.

Our walk of faith in God is much like that. The psalmist wrote: ***"Thy word is a lamp unto my feet and a light unto my path"*** (Psalm 119:105). God illuminates our path one step at a time, one turn at a time. One thing I realized about the GPS in my car: if the voice stopped speaking and I really had no idea where I was going, I was lost. And that is how I felt many times over the 15 years as I continued to wait on the Lord. I knew I was in His will, but I didn't have all the information I felt I needed readily available to me. And yet, through it all, His grace was there, working in my life in such a way that allowed me to walk out those years one step at a time, one act of obedience at a time. His grace kept me from becoming anxious and making rash decisions that were rooted in fear. I found a place inside that grace that anchored me in Him, and I grew to understand that this is how God gets the maximum glory out of a life.

As I sat in that hotel room in Montreal, these words came to me—words I later set to music:

Let me be lost in Your will; found in Your grace
Holding Your hand; seeking Your face;
Let me be anchored in the safety of Your secret place.
Lost in Your will; found in Your grace
I know You love me
And everything You plan for me is for my good.
Your ways are much higher than I could ever imagine.
So I've learned to put my trust in You;
I've learned to keep my eyes on You!

I truly believe that God works this same way in the life of every believer. He's working this same way in your life, leading you one step at a time, one act of obedience at a time. Just trust Him! Know how much He loves you and never doubt His intentions for you. Rely on His all-sufficient grace. Listen for the voice of Holy Spirit (your internal GPS), whispering, "This is the way; walk in it!" Know with assurance that Voice will lead you to your expected end and into a deeper, more intimate relationship with the Lord.

Chapter 12

Trust the God of the Process

And we know that God causes all things to work together for good to those who love God, to those who are called according to His purpose.
Romans 8:28

God's purposes, His plans, as well as His methods are beyond what we may see or comprehend. He is the God who declares the end from the beginning (Isaiah 46:10); He knows His intended outcome for each season of our lives. He knows the next place of faith He has for us, and He prepares us for that next place in advance. He uses everything situation, every challenge, every choice, every experience—the good and the bad—and causes them to work in symphony for our good and His purposes. No experience is wasted; it's all preparation. We may not always recognize it as preparation because we are focused on the now, focused on the need. But God is working beyond the moment we're in; He's working beyond the current need. I look back now and know that those 15 years were about more than my physical healing and wholeness.

Once you and I have decided to live in the realm of ridiculous faith and not simply visit from time to time, the Lord will create unique opportunities for us to trust Him in greater, grander, more ridiculous ways. Each time we unrelentingly stand on His Word, choosing to obey Him at all costs, we are positioned to know Him in ways we've not known before. As we journey deeper into this new place of faith, we discover that the Father orchestrates and uses each experience to teach us something about His love, His grace, and His power. With each victory, we become more deeply rooted in Him, in His Word, and in His covenant promises. Each victory strengthens our faith and opens our eyes to see greater possibilities as we continue to grow. Each victory of faith enables us to believe for the "ridiculous" if we are willing to embrace and live out the lessons learned at each juncture of our walk. Those lessons are our steppingstones into the next place of faith and grace.

We see this evidenced in the life of Abraham. Each test, each challenge allowed him to know more of the God who had called him into a marvelous covenant relationship. Each victory strengthened Abraham's faith. By the time God tells him to sacrifice Isaac, Abraham's confidence in the Lord is so settled that he doesn't hesitate. Abraham knew that Jehovah God was the covenant-keeping God. He knew that the same God who'd promised a son, the same God who brought forth that son, was the same God who would resurrect that son, if necessary, to fulfill the covenant. Abraham didn't get to that place overnight. And God used every experience to mature Abraham and establish him in absolute faith.

> **With each victory, we become more deeply rooted in Him, in His Word, and in His covenant promises. Each victory strengthens our faith and opens our eyes to see greater possibilities as we continue to grow.**

Through our experiences, challenges, and tests, God reveals the potential, wisdom, gifts, talents, and strengths He has deposited in us as well as those things in our lives that may hinder our progress. He reveals any areas in our thinking that stop us from fully embracing our true identity in Him. The Lord reveals the fears, the insecurities, the wounds from our past, the habits and patterns in our lives that we may not even be aware exist. He reveals those things because He wants us free of anything that robs us of the abundant life Christ gives. God wants us free from anything that prevents us from walking out purpose and fulfilling destiny or causes us to take the convenient way out.

Magnificent Glory

"I realize that, in and of myself, if I am not completely yielded and totally surrendered, my flesh, my mind, my reason, my will, my intellect will

always lean towards the lesser version of a more powerful, more magnificent glory that He is worthy of and that He is after!"

I found myself writing these words as I reflected on my journey, the pathway and the process to healing. There were times during those 15 years that I was presented with options that offered a convenient out. Uncertainty can cause us to consider other options. Had I taken another path, made another decision, chosen what was easiest and most convenient, I would have been settling for a lesser version of God's glory. That's the difference between us *giving* God glory and God *getting* the glory out of our lives.

Let's face it. No one steps in this realm of faith intentionally choosing the most difficult, the most challenging path. No one opts for pain or loss; no one opts for years of waiting; no one opts for uncertainty. It's human nature to want the easiest, most convenient solution. When we become weary and anxious, we may seek and then choose a more convenient way out without even realizing that's what we're doing. And believe me, the enemy of your soul is watching, listening, and waiting for the perfect opportunity to present you with those convenient options. He's after your faith, and if he can't bring you to a place of doubt and unbelief, he will attempt to keep God from getting the maximum glory by offering you an out. When we are unable to comprehend the path and process God employs, those options become appealing. They give us a sense of control and certainty. And all too often, we don't even realize what we are choosing.

Even though Abraham believed the promises of God, he didn't fully understand the path and the processes of God. Keep in mind, Abraham was still discovering who God was and still growing in his trust and faith. We may be surprised at some of the choices Abraham made along the way, but he is no different than we are. On more than one occasion, when presented with a convenient way, Abraham chose it. He lied, not once but twice, about his relationship with Sarah (Genesis 12 and 20). Ten years after receiving the promise of an heir, when Sarah suggested he sire a child with her maiden, Abraham agreed (Genesis 16). He chose a culturally accepted practice; Hagar became a convenient way out. But God's path and His process were designed to produce something greater than Abraham—or you and I—could ever produce through the flesh.

As we study Abraham's life, we see a pattern. I believe God used each circumstance in Abraham's life—from famine to Lot and Hagar—to allow Abraham to see his weaknesses and his propensity to make decisions rooted in an old way of thinking and in what he'd been taught was acceptable within his culture. The Lord was revealing to Abraham his tendency to choose the convenient way out and, therefore, opt for a lesser version of God's glory in his life.

> *The Lord was revealing to Abraham his tendency to choose the convenient way out and, therefore, opt for a lesser version of God's glory in his life.*

The Lord wanted to break those patterns of thinking that led to patterns of behavior in Abraham. He wanted Abraham to fully trust His Word, His will, and His way through the total surrender of Abraham's own will and way. Ultimately, the Lord wanted all those associated with Abraham—his family, servants, the other inhabitants in the land—to see His power and glory undeniably displayed. Then all would know Jehovah as the true and living God. That is God's desire for you and me.

Free Me from Me

While walking through my health journey, I was still intentional in my pursuit of purpose and destiny, not only in my life but also for the church and those joined to our local fellowship. The years following the procedure in Montreal were years of navigating through how to get to the next place that would produce a greater manifestation of God's glory. I had come to a place of not wanting to settle for less than God intended. I had come to the place of not wanting to take the convenient way out—no matter what that meant.

It was also a season of the Lord setting me free from self-imposed limitations—those limitations we place on ourselves that stem from our past experiences and that are often rooted in fear. They are limits that have been set based on the way we think about ourselves or our surroundings. They are usually thoughts of being inferior, inadequate, or unprepared. They are thoughts that lead to feelings of intimidation, fear of rejection, fear of failure, and insecurities. They are thoughts and feelings that, once brought down, reveal the basis for them was false and unfounded.

Holy Spirit revealed things from my upbringing, things that had been spoken to me or about me, and how I had been treated that had caused me to create limitations in my thinking. They were now impacting how I walked out my faith. He showed me patterns and habits in my life that could impede my progress and cause me to live a small life rather than live the life He had purposed for me. Once they'd been revealed, Holy Spirit helped me overcome them—one action, one step, one circumstance at a time—preparing me for His next invitation and that place of the greater glory. The same God who continually sets me free does the same for you.

Are you being presented with an opportunity, an invitation to experience the greater glory, but because the path is obscure and the process is unknown, you are willing to take the convenient way out? That way out may lessen the price you must pay, the level of sacrifice you must make, the level of suffering you must endure, all of which tie into that greater glory God wants to get out of your life. When you choose the out, you forfeit so much more. God is preparing you for even greater things. Know that His presence, His grace, His power, His love, His favor are with you, and you will see His glory if you simply stay the course.

Chapter 13

Are You Waiting, or Have You Quit?

Your ears will hear a word behind you, saying, "This is the way, walk in it," whenever you turn to the right or to the left.
Isaiah 30:21

"You quit!"

The words jolted me. They came during the morning session of a conference in South Africa in 2015. I had traveled there with my pastor, Bishop Joseph L. Garlington and his Reconciliation team, and that day he called me to the platform. "I have a word for you," he said and began to share a word from the Lord that would change my life, challenge me to walk in greater manifestation of faith, and settle me more deeply in the realm of ridiculous faith.

There are times in our walk with the Lord that we may sincerely believe we are operating in a place of faith when we are not. We convince ourselves that we are waiting on God, but in reality, we have stopped. We have given up, and most often, it's because of fear. We are not completely free of our self-imposed limitations; we question whether we can do what God is calling us to do; we are unable to see ourselves as God sees us. As a result, we may reduce the vision God has given us. We allow ourselves to become comfortable where we are even though we know that God has so much more for us. We rationalize our action (or inaction), never really recognizing or acknowledging that we just stopped.

I'd unknowingly landed in that place, and the Lord lovingly and graciously chastened me that morning. I had to acknowledge that while I'd said to the Lord, "I am waiting on You," I had become satisfied and settled, both physically and mentally, in a place that was too small for the vision God had given.

"This is the season," Bishop continued, "for you not to cast away your confidence, but with vision and vigilance and aggressiveness, go back to the place where you quit and just say, 'God, I'm just going to stay right here until You reign! I'm going to stay right here until You fulfill the promise that You made to me!'" That morning God called me to a place of repentance. He said, "*Now take the wraps off. Take the wraps off because I'm coming, and I want you to be ready when I come.*" God was up to something amazing, and He was encouraging me to get back up, to stand in faith, and move forward.

> *There are times in our walk with the Lord that we may sincerely believe we are operating in a place of faith when we are not. We convince ourselves that we are waiting on God, but in reality, we have stopped.*

God had spoken. I had to respond—not just in word but in action.

Faith in Uncertainty

I'd known long before that trip to South Africa our church needed to move from the space we'd been leasing. We'd outgrown the space, and statistics show that once a church reaches a certain threshold, there will be a decline if it doesn't adjust. We were beginning to see that decline. For us to step into the next level of ministry God had for us, I knew we'd have to make a physical move. And while I had begun looking at other locations, I had not resolved to do whatever it took to make that move happen. I was grappling with uncertainty. I needed to regain confidence in my ability to know God's voice. And I admit that there was some fear of failing.

When it came time to renew our lease, I opted to renew, in part, because of the uncertainties. I'd convinced myself we were good right where we were. And yet, I was not at all satisfied with things as they were. The vision I had for Heirs had always been bigger, grander, greater than the 10,000 square-foot space we occupied. But I had allowed my self-imposed limitations to keep me from transitioning to that next place. I had become stagnant. I was teaching on ridiculous faith but not extending my faith to the same degree I encouraged others.

It's not unlike the children of Israel. They had seen the power of

God and His faithfulness to honor His covenant over and over again. Even while they were in Egypt, we are told that they *"were fruitful and increased abundantly, multiplied and grew exceedingly mighty…"* and that the more the Egyptians afflicted them, the stronger they grew (Exodus 1:7, 12). When they cried out to God, the Bible tells us He heard them, remembered His covenant, and set His plan in motion to deliver them (Exodus 2:23-25). We know the story of the plagues, the miraculous exodus, the parting of the Red Sea, and all the incredible ways God protected and provided for them. Their trust in Him should have been unshakeable. And yet, on more than one occasion, they cried to return to the bondage from which God had delivered them. Why would they want to go back to enslavement rather than trust God to get them the Promised Land? Uncertainty.

> *Change and transition always come with an inherent "dynamic of uncertainty" that can unsettle the best of us. People will remain in or return to a situation—even a bad one— rather than face uncertainty.*

You see, change and transition always come with an inherent "dynamic of uncertainty" that can unsettle the best of us. People will remain in or return to a situation—even a bad one— rather than face uncertainty. We prefer the familiar and often choose to live small lives instead of contending for all God has promised because of our need for certainty. That is what we see with the children of Israel. God had promised them a land flowing with milk and honey, but they would have opted for bondage rather than face uncertainty.

> *If we are unwilling to surrender our need for certainty and place absolute, unrelenting trust in God, we can get stuck and comfortable in that small way of thinking and living.*

They failed to see that the same God who had miraculously brought them out of Egypt was the same God who would lead them to the land He'd promised. It sounds insane, but you and I often do the same thing. We choose to stay in a small place—physically, mentally, spiritually, relationally—or we choose to return to a familiar place that is much less than God intends for us because we do not want to weather the winds of uncertainty that come with change and transition. If we are unwilling to surrender our need for certainty and place absolute, unrelenting trust in God, we can get stuck and comfortable in that small way of thinking and living. We must realize that faith is the neutralizer of fear and the stabilizer of the unknown.

God loves us too much to allow us to stay stuck. He wants us to know His intentions for us are always good. If He calls us to step into a place that seems foreign to us, if He calls us to "enlarge the place of our tent," He will guide us to our destination. And when we get stuck, God will often do whatever it takes to get our attention and move us forward in His purposes and plans—even if it means taking us to the other side of the globe so we can hear Him speak.

Embracing the Prophetic

One of the keys to living in the realm of ridiculous faith is remaining sensitive to the voice of God. As we read in Isaiah 30:21, the Lord desires to lead us by His voice, to direct us by His Word. You and I must understand that our fears and self-imposed limitations can impact our ability to hear His voice clearly. I'd stopped moving because I'd stopped listening. I'd somehow lost confidence in my ability to hear Him, and He spoke to me through Bishop Garlington and through others to shake me from that place. For months following, others came to me with similar words: "*Stop holding back! It's time to let go and be all God intended you to be.*" Through the prophetic words spoken to me in that season, I was able to move from my comfort zone to the point of no return.

> **God wants us to make progress in Him. He wants us to succeed. He wants us to advance, and in so doing, advance His Kingdom.**

If we are to live in this new realm of faith, you and I must be willing to embrace the prophetic. We see throughout Scripture that God would send His prophets to speak to His people. He'd speak to them of their need to repent and the consequences if they did not. He'd speak concerning His purposes and plans for them, to encourage them to trust Him, to encourage them to move forward with their eyes on Him. He'd speak to comfort them and to strengthen them. He'd speak to warn them and to give strategy. When they received the word of the Lord through the prophets, they fared well; when they rejected the word, they suffered dire consequences.

Second Chronicles 20:20b instructs us to *"Believe in the Lord your God, and you shall be established; believe His prophets, and you shall prosper."* The promise is that if we believe God, we will be firmly rooted. If we believe His prophets, we will prosper. The Hebrew word for "prosper" means advancing, making progress, being profitable, succeeding. God wants us to make progress in Him. He wants us to succeed. He wants us to advance, and in so doing, advance His Kingdom. Through prophetic words, we can know God's heart, His purposes and plans beyond what we can see in the moment. When He speaks, even if it is a challenging word to hear, we want to receive the word rather than reject or reduce it. Then we must resolve in our hearts to act in faith on the word we have received.

> *Through prophetic words, we can know God's heart, His purposes and plans beyond that which we can see in the moment.*

Increased Capacity

When I returned to the States, I called my leadership team together. "This is not me," I said as I pointed around the sanctuary. "This does not represent what God has placed in my heart. God has allowed me to travel and minister in various places globally, and I come home, and things don't match. Things don't add up." Then I shared the prophetic word I'd received, acknowledged that I had stopped, and I wept as I repented. As the apostle and senior pastor, my stopping had impacted everyone else's progress. I not only repented to my leaders but also to our congregation.

The Lord gave me a message entitled "My Capacity Has Increased: Don't Believe Me, Just Watch!" I preached that message and then gave myself to walking out what God had placed in my heart.

You may be looking at your current situation and thinking, "This is not what I envisioned! This does not represent me!" I want to encourage you to seek God and ask Him if you have stopped. Have you said, "I'm waiting on the Lord," but in reality, you quit? If so, take a moment right now and repent. Ask God to forgive you and then get up and start moving again. Look for Him to open doors of opportunity for you to exercise your faith once again!

A few months later, on a flight home from a ministry trip to Singapore, I opened my email and found the Prophetic Bulletin by Bill and Marsha Burns. As I read, I knew it was yet another word from the Lord to encourage me. It confirmed all He'd been speaking to me. It read, in part:

"I say to you right now, I know your heart and that your heart is for Me. Understand that I will not forsake you. Never will I leave you. For, I am leading you to a fresh pasture. I'm leading you to new ground. I'm leading you into the place of My Glory, even in these days. And it begins this very moment and this time that as you realize that I am one with you that you will know that everything is going to be okay. Just walk. Walk with Me. Believe in Me... The transition that you are in at this time is not a simple transition between seasons of your life but is a transition from one era to another. It is more significant than you have realized. What is coming in the next span of time will, in many ways, bring to fruition that which you have worked for in the past decade. ("The Trumpet" and "Small Straws in the Soft Wind," May 15, 2015)

Swift Obedience

Faith takes action. Faith moves. Even in our uncertainty, our movement tells God we believe Him, and He honors that. I've said it before, but it bears repeating: God would rather see us move out in *some* direction and redirect us, if necessary, than to see us sit still and claim we are "waiting" on Him. Sometimes He's simply waiting on us. As we move, we can expect things and people to move as well. As we move out, we can expect doors of opportunity to open.

As I actively began looking for the place God had for us, doors did open. It would be wonderful to tell you the first place we looked at was the right place. It wasn't. We looked at purchasing the property where we were, but that didn't come together. We looked at the property next door and a church only a few blocks away. Nothing came together. As we journey in the realm of ridiculous faith, there may be times when it looks like "hits and misses."

When we believe that God is directing us and things don't happen as we thought they would, we run the risk of stopping. But that's the time when we must be all the more diligent in exercising our faith to its fullest capacity. We must anchor ourselves in Hebrews 10:35, and not cast away our confidence, and keep moving.

Faith takes action. Faith moves. Even in our uncertainty, our movement tells God that we believe Him, and He honors that.

Let's look again at Isaac. We read in Genesis 26 that he'd dig wells in one place only for his enemies to come and claim the wells. But he didn't stop digging; he kept moving and digging until he landed in the place God had for him. He named that place Rehoboth, meaning "the Lord has Made Room for Us."

God would rather see us move out in some direction and redirect us if necessary than to see us sit still and claim we are "waiting" on Him.

What a wonderful example Isaac is for us! Don't quit. Don't stop. Even if there is contention, even if it seems nothing is working, keep going. Keep believing. Keep digging! The same God that made room for Isaac is the same God who will make room for you.

God did just that for us, and almost a year after I received that prophetic word, we moved to a new facility with greater opportunity to expand, fulfill the vision, impact lives, and advance God's Kingdom.

And with the move came another invitation to move even further into the realm of ridiculous faith.

Chapter 14

A Season of Contradiction

With all this going for us, my dear, dear friends, stand your ground. And don't hold back. Throw yourselves into the work of the Master, confident that nothing you do for him is a waste of time or effort.
1 Corinthians 15:58 The Message

We have seen that one key to not only living in the realm of ridiculous faith but moving to greater heights is remaining consistent in our faith walk. Consistency is defined as "steadfast adherence to the same principles or course." It is synonymous with steadfastness, congruency, stability. I believe that is what the Apostle Paul meant when he wrote, **"Therefore, my beloved brothers and sisters, be firm, immovable, always excelling in the work of the Lord, knowing that your labor is not in vain in the Lord"** (1 Corinthians 15:58).

He is encouraging us to remain consistent because consistency in faith brings great reward. God honors our consistency. That is why we must not shrink back. We must not waver. Remaining steadfast in our pursuit of the Lord and all He has spoken to us allows us to see its manifestation. Until the Lord says otherwise, we must be willing to stay the course—no matter how challenging it may seem or how much it may seem to contradict the word we've received from Him. Even in seasons of seeming contradiction, God is working in us and preparing us for our "next."

One reality of life in the realm of ridiculous faith is that more is required of us with each opportunity God gives. A greater level of faith. A greater level of endurance. A greater reliance on God's grace. A greater level of resolve and determination. Why? Because we will also face a greater level of resistance and testing.

An Opportunity to Grow Together

The prophetic word I received in South Africa had settled my resolve. I was determined to demonstrate that I'd received the word. I would, by faith, do my part. An opportunity opened for us to share a facility with another congregation. They had wanted to sell the property, but after some discussion with the pastor and his Board, we entered an agreement to share the building with them. After five years, we would purchase the property outright. The church building was 67,000 square feet and sat on 13 acres of land. Even though the building needed work, it was large enough for us to do what we envisioned. It was an incredible opportunity for two fellowships—one predominately White and the other predominantly Black—to work together to change the community and demonstrate the Kingdom of God in more significant ways.

> *One reality of life in the realm of ridiculous faith is that more is required of us with each opportunity God gives.*

In March 2016—Resurrection Sunday—we held our first service in our new home. We were excited about all the possibilities and did all we could to collaborate with the other congregation's leadership and members. We held joint services in which our worship teams ministered as one team, and the pastor and I alternated speaking. We merged our children's ministries. We worked on outreach projects together. We planned get-togethers so the leadership of both churches could get to know each other. We jointly hosted events. Heirs contributed to the beautification of the building, helped with some of the much-needed repairs, and purchased items that benefitted both congregations. We sensed that God desired to do something unprecedented that would have a lasting impact beyond the city's borders. And as we put forth the effort for unity, God did some wonderful things in building relationships between many of the people. I knew that this was not about a piece of property. God was doing something of Kingdom proportions.

Unrealized Expectation

When God speaks a word to you concerning purpose, calling, and destiny, and you embrace that word by faith, you may expect things to go a certain way. After all, God has given you a vision. You know you may face some challenges in the process of obtaining the promise, but you can see an expected outcome, and the challenges don't halt you. You roll up your sleeves and prepare to do all that the Lord says. You know you are walking in His power, His grace, and His truth. You step into that new space. Things aren't perfect, but they seem to be heading in the right direction. And then things shift. The reality is far from the expectation.

There are times when you make a decision that doesn't play out the way you thought it would. You may be tempted to believe you've missed God. Just because it doesn't work out as you anticipated doesn't mean God wasn't in it. It is all a part of the journey; it's all a part of you becoming the person God created you to be. God uses what is unexpected to you to mature you, strengthen you, and build your endurance and spiritual stamina, to establish you.

The enemy, however, wants you to doubt your choices and doubt your ability to hear and recognize God's voice. Do you know that the devil trembles at the thought of you learning to live in this new place of faith? He'd prefer you remain on the periphery rather than enter the realm of ridiculous faith. He knows the further you go into that realm, the more dangerous you become, and he will do whatever he can to stop you from acting on the word of Lord for your life, to stop you from standing on the promise and seeing the completed work.

> *There are times when you make a decision that doesn't play out the way you thought it would. You may be tempted to believe you've missed God. Just because it doesn't work out as you anticipated doesn't mean God wasn't in it.*

Before we moved, I'd spent time casting vision and helping the members of Heirs dream big. I wanted them to know our new location was the place that they would be able to do the things God had spoken to them—in some cases, things that had been on hold for years. This was the place they'd have greater Kingdom impact, greater Kingdom influence, and see greater Kingdom results. I knew that we'd lose a few members because of the move; that's bound to happen. But I believed our congregation would grow and that those who remained would have opportunity to use the gifts and talents God had placed in them in new and fresh ways.

I wasn't going in expecting there'd be no challenges. The Lord had told me to get on the grounds and not focus on the giants, with the promise that His Presence and His blessing would be evident. I knew we'd have to make some adjustments. We'd be stretched and we'd have some obstacles to overcome. Initially, things seemed to go well. But it became increasingly apparent that, while many from the other congregation welcomed us and were eager to work together, others saw us as mere "renters" rather than partners in ministry. Some were resistant to change, and that included some in leadership. And though we extended ourselves to make things work, to say our time there was challenging would be an understatement.

> *God will always make His presence known in the realm of ridiculous faith. In the midst of the challenges, if you and I focus on the Lord, remaining aware of His presence, we can overcome the difficulties.*

God honored His word, and the one thing that remained constant the two years we shared the building was His Presence and blessing. One of the things that we see in the lives of Abraham, Isaac, Jacob, Joseph, and so many others is the manifest presence of God. God will always make His presence known in the realm of ridiculous faith. In the midst of the challenges, if you and I focus on the Lord, remaining aware of His presence, we can overcome the difficulties.

Firm in Faith

I recognized that there was a deeper work God wanted to do in me and those in our congregation during that period. It was a season for me to really be all He'd created me to be—unapologetically so. I was determined to, first and foremost, honor God in all I did. I learned the importance of taking a posture of humility before Him and being quick to repent. I learned how to speak the truth in love, even when it wasn't received. I chose not to complain, continue to speak faith-filled words, and allow Holy Spirit to lead. During difficulties, I continued to worship the Lord as I always had, to teach and preach the Word as I always had. I was determined not to relent.

In his first epistle, the Apostle Peter tells us that we are to humble ourselves under the hand of God and cast our cares on Him, knowing He cares for us. Peter goes on to tell us that the devil roams like a lion seeking prey to devour. Then the apostle writes:

So resist him, firm in your faith, knowing that the same experiences of suffering are being accomplished by your brothers and sisters who are in the world. After you have suffered for a little while, the God of all grace, who called you to His eternal glory in Christ, will Himself perfect, confirm, strengthen, and establish you. To Him be dominion forever and ever. Amen **(1 Peter 5:9-11).**

This must be your posture when things around you are the very antithesis of what God has spoken. You must not give any room for the enemy to swoop in and move you from your position of faith. He will take advantage of every opportunity you give. I learned the importance of continually yielding to the Lord to avoid becoming offended or reacting in situations designed by the enemy to harm me, harm the ministry, and destroy the witness.

You must learn to do the same. Be quick to repent, to forgive, and seek reconciliation. Always keep your eyes on the Lord. I know that's not always easy; our flesh is eager to react. But know God's grace is always available to you. Rely on that grace. Surrender and allow the fruit of the Spirit to manifest in your life (Galatians 5:22,23). God is at work in you and will establish you both in the spirit and the natural.

> *You must not give any room for the enemy to swoop in and move you from your position of faith.*

Realize this: *Every promise, every word the Lord speaks to you will be tested.* Remember the story of Joseph? He dreamed that his father and brothers would bow before him. But before the dream became a reality, he was sold into slavery by his brothers, lied on by Potiphar's wife, imprisoned, and forgotten. It was a season of contradiction for Joseph. Psalm 105 gives us this insight:

He sent a man before them—
Joseph—who was sold as a slave.
They hurt his feet with fetters,
He was laid in irons.
<u>Until the time that his word came to pass,</u>
<u>The word of the Lord tested him.</u>
Psalm 105:17-19 (NKJV emphasis added)

The New American Standard Bible says the word of the Lord "refined" him. The word will test us and remove any impurities in us. That's what refining does. It removes anything in us that is not like God, anything that can hinder us from stepping humbly into the place God has prepared for us, anything that distorts His image in us. Refining requires fire. We must endure the heat. Through yielding to the Lord, giving Holy Spirit full reign, and receiving God's grace, we will respond to the testing according to the Word and not our flesh.

I'm convinced that Joseph focused on the Lord during his time in the pit, in Potiphar's house, and in prison. He was able to remain in that "secret place" and that's how he endured and eventually overcame. We read over and over again that the Lord was with Joseph, and he always found favor wherever he was. In times of testing, in less-than-desirable conditions, the enemy would have us focus on the circumstances or ourselves. But if we are to experience God's Presence and His continual blessing and favor, if we are to see that which God has spoken come to pass, we must keep our eyes on Him and our ears attentive to His voice. Trust that God will honor His word as He continues to refine you. Keep your focus on Him!

Those years were difficult. My leaders were sometimes treated as if they were irrelevant. It some cases, our members were not made to feel significant or welcomed, and some even stopped attending services. Efforts to make our presence known were resisted. Soon the joint services stopped. I had led people there with the promise that things would shift, only to be met with resistance and given limitations that made it difficult for us do what we desired to do with the level of excellence we were used to. There were some difficult and discouraging conversations, and I would make every effort to quickly reconcile. And while I knew we were all being tested, I did not want to see my congregation hurt, dishonored, or disregarded in any way. I had learned over the years to endure; I had learned to stand on God's word until He said otherwise.

But often that posture affected others. Was my willingness to stand on the word of God causing our members to suffer needlessly? Would more leave as a result? Had I misunderstood what God had spoken? Had I led those I was called to cover and protect into the wilderness? I admit, I questioned the decision to share the space. The spirit of discouragement tried to latch on to me.

We weren't even a year into our five-year agreement, and I wasn't sure what the next four years would look like. I knew if there wasn't a shift, we could lose more members. The change I had promised was not becoming a reality and the disappointment was palpable. I needed to hear from God.

In January of 2017, I traveled again to Covenant Church of Pittsburgh for their "Times of Refreshing," and there the Lord spoke to me just what I needed to get my second wind. My last day in Pittsburgh, I received prophetic ministry from my pastors, Bishop Joseph and Pastor Barbara Garlington, and other prophets at the conference. I received words concerning property and a title deed, which I will share in more detail later. The words from Pastor Barbara, from Bishop, and another dear brother caused the spirit of discouragement to lift and brought hope.

He [the Lord] said tell John that I'm about to do some things in his house and I'm about to change mindsets and hearts. And I'm about to bring unity and understanding even on the home front. I'm going to bring a new day, a new season, a new light, a new life. I'm going to lift this weight off you, Son...I'm going to lift it off you now. I'm going to lift it off you, says the Lord.

I'm going to lift the weight off you. I'm going to lift the feeling that you have that 'I'm out here all by myself. I'm fighting alone.' God says, Son, you're not fighting alone. I'm with you. I'm in the battle with you and I'm going to pull all the pieces together... And I'm not going to let the devil destroy even My ground and the territory that I gave you, says God. I'm going to bring unity and I'm going to change minds. I'm going to change hearts. I'm going to bring peace back to you.

Sometimes you've said, in the last month or so, 'Lord, I don't know how much of this I can take.' I'm going to take it with you. I'm going to carry it for you now...Now I'm going to love you and train you and teach you and father you, says the Lord. For I came to lift you up! I came to lift you up out of the doldrums of heaviness, out of the fear and discouragement. I come to take discouragement off of you. Off of you. Heaviness in the heart of a man makes it stoop, but a good word makes it glad.

I knew it was the Lord speaking to me. No one knew the weight I was feeling during that time—no one but God. Pastor Barbara spoke:

John, this is a turning point for you to trust God in a way that you've never had to before. It's like the prophet told us last week: our future is where we're going. It's not where we're starting, but we're going to meet it because God's already prepared it. And so the worship and the praise is going to be the thing to help you understand. This is a season of teaching and learning for you. It's the season that's going to promote you into another position that you're going to be able to see things you've never seen before. You're going to be able to help people in ways you've never helped them before. We think that our testings are coming from the devil but many times they're coming from God. God uses everything to make us what He's already called us to be.

And Bishop Garlington sealed it.

There's a song that we've been singing for years and as it bubbles up in my spirit, I think of you, that your journey in God has taken you in various places and once in a while it's taken you off the path. But you've always come back to it. But the deep desire of your heart really hasn't been for fame; it hasn't been for fortune. People know your name. So when we sing "You're all I want; You're all I've ever needed," that's the cry of your heart. And I hear God saying: "You're all I want." And though we like to

> *say God doesn't need anything, He can send someone and say, "Tell John, I have need of him."*
>
> *There is so much of you in this house and people have no idea how much of you is here. We sing your songs and people just say, "That's one of our songs" and they don't really know. You listen to the word and God gives you a song that takes the message where it would never go without the song. But in your worship, in your praise, in your steadfastness, you've reached the tipping point. It's done! You've pushed and pushed, and it's come to that axiom, that place where it can't do anything but fall over. Thank you, Jesus.*
>
> *There's a shifting. There is a shifting. There's a turning.*

All I could do was weep. Once again, the Lord had demonstrated His love for me. The Apostle Paul tells us in 1 Corinthians 14:3 that prophesy is to encourage, edify, and comfort us. I had received the encouragement and edification I needed to walk through the season of contradiction. I prayed that those in our congregation would recognize the season we were in and endure the refining until the promise was fulfilled.

You will walk through seasons of contradiction. You may find yourself in one right now. How do you know? A season of contradiction is:
- *A time when everything seems to go the opposite way.*
- *A time that tests your belief in God's Word and His ability to perform it.*
- *A time that tests and builds your faith in God's Word.*
- *A time that produces conviction and commitment to God.*
- *A time that produces greater trust and obedience.*

You must realize it is only a season, and seasons end. Every winter gives way to Spring. If you remain focused on the Lord, worship Him, resist the need to control the situation, resist the temptation to act hastily, and silence the voice of the enemy by rehearsing the promises of God for your life, you will in time step into a season of fulfillment that will amaze you.

Chapter 15

Passing the Test

For our light affliction, which is but for a moment, is working for us a far more exceeding and eternal weight of glory...
2 Corinthians 4:17

Jesus had uttered His last words, "It is finished." Then the Bible tells is He "gave up the ghost." I imagine at that moment those who had followed Him felt lost, hopeless. They'd believed Jesus would overthrow Roman rule. They'd believed He would establish His Kingdom here on earth. And even though Jesus spent three years teaching them about the Kingdom of God and what it looked like, they didn't get it. He explained why He'd come and predicted both His death and resurrection. They didn't get it. They were dismayed as He took His last breath on the cross. The men on the road to Emmaus even said, "We were hoping it was He who was going to redeem Israel" (Luke 24:21). Because they didn't fully understand how He would redeem not only Israel but the world, they landed in a place of despair. He was their hope, and now He was gone.

Often when the Lord speaks to us—either directly or through others—about our destiny and what He has planned for us, we attempt to place that prophetic word in our current context or a context that makes sense to us. Rarely does it fit. Just like the first followers of Christ, what we think God means and what He has actually purposed to do can be worlds apart. You see, we only understand in part. We only see in part. When the word of the Lord doesn't line up with our understanding of it, we must not dismiss it or allow ourselves to sink into a place of hopelessness. God is drawing us into His context. We must allow Him to bring the understanding we need, continue to move in faith and allow the Word to unfold before us.

A Change of Perspective

While I was in Pittsburgh that January of 2017, I received the following word from my brother and prophet from South Africa, Ron Campbell:

> *Now John, I don't know what's going on in the natural, but while he was praying for you, the spirit of the Lord told me that this battle is about title, and a stronghold has risen up against the ownership of property. And today that stronghold wants to resist you being able to enter into the place that God has promised for you. It's the giants that are in the land. Today God says, "Watch how I go, and I destroy this giant, and I move this barricade out the way." So, Father, today we release the power. Lord, You promised that there would be ownership of land and there would be a title presented, and today, Lord, the battle has been about ownership of land and title as well as having authority in that region. And so, Father, I thank You today that You are the one who will conquer that stronghold. There's a spirit of greed that has risen up against you. I just break the power of that thing right now. And I send the word and I pray, Lord, for redemption of this land and redemption of this title. I thank You today, Father, a supernatural shift will come and move the barricade out the way. And the Lord told me to tell you "Do not fear." In Jesus' name.*

God had told us to get on the grounds; we did. He'd said not to focus on the giants in the land; we didn't, as challenging as that was. Now He was letting me know that there was a fight for the land, and that settled something in me. We were where we were supposed to be, and though it would be a fight, it wasn't my fight. It was the Lord's, and He always wins! He would fulfill His word. We simply needed to stand and not lose faith. We needed to allow the word to unfold as God intended, not as we'd envisioned it. We'd walk through the season of contradiction, remembering His faithfulness to us in the past, knowing that He was more than able to do what He'd promised.

I'd seen the fulfillment of that word in a specific context. I'd believed the land He was talking about was the land we were currently on. God was about to pull me into His context and open my eyes to things beyond our current location. He'd soon draw me into a deeper place of ridiculous faith. The land and the title deed He promised would be ours if we did not give in or give up.

Welcome Back

Things didn't get better, but I was fortified by the word I'd received. God released a grace to walk through the season of contradiction. I could not control the actions of others. I could not control the perception or choices of others. I could control my response. I chose to continue to preach the word, live my convictions, stand firm in who I knew God had created me to be. I prayed that others got a glimpse of what God was doing for us and in us during this season of contradiction.

It was during that period I began teaching this message on ridiculous faith. I'd taught it years before, but God had started to give me greater revelation, I believe, in part, because of my willingness to repent (change) and, in part, because He knew what was ahead for me and our body. As I taught the series, I could sense a change *in* me. And then God did something *for* me as a sign of His approval.

One of the ladies in our congregation was looking to buy a car. Mutual acquaintances were selling an older model Mercedes, and she'd sent me a picture to get my thoughts. "It's a nice car," I texted back, adding, "I'd buy that!"

She decided not to purchase it, but mentioned to the owners that I was interested (which is not exactly what I'd said), and they reached out to me. I wasn't in the market for a car (I quite liked the payment-free Lexus I was driving), but I thought there could be no harm in looking at it. We arranged to meet in the parking lot of Heirs' previous location. The car needed to be cleaned up, but it was in mint condition.

"I believe the Lord wants you to have this car," the owner said.

"How much are you asking for it?" I inquired. When he told me the price, I told him I didn't have the resources readily available to make that kind of purchase.

"Well, why don't you drive it for a while. See if you like, and we'll talk some more."

I drove the car for two days and liked it but reiterated to the owner when we spoke again that I didn't have the funds at that time.

"We really believe that this car is for you," he said.

We met again in the same parking lot. I had every intention of returning the car to him to find that he had signed the title over to me!

"I trust you. I believe whenever you have the money, you'll give it to us. We're going to sign it over to you!"

At that time, my daughter, Leslie, wanted an automobile. I'd given her a car years before and had purchased a Lexus. Leslie, by faith, had claimed my car. "Dad," she'd said, "when you're done with this car, I want you to give it to me." I believe the Lord created an opportunity for me to receive a car to bless my daughter with what she wanted. Sometimes the exercising of your faith is the answer to someone else's prayer.

> **Sometimes the exercising of your faith is the answer to someone else's prayer.**

"I want to bless you with a car," I told her. I'd cleaned out the Lexus and put my belongings in the Mercedes. I picked up my daughter, drove to that same parking lot, and she drove off with the Lexus.

As I was pulling out of the lot in the Mercedes, I heard Holy Spirit say, *"Welcome back!"* I immediately knew what He was saying. *"Welcome back to that place you were in when you received the Mercedes from Jim Martin. Welcome back to the realm of ridiculous faith."*

Passing the Test

"Absolutely not!"

That was the response when we'd met with the pastor. We wanted to purchase the property for the balance of the loan and continue to share the space and work together with the other congregation. But he was convinced that his Board would not agree to sell on those terms. At that moment, I heard the Lord say, *"You're done!"* It was clear that it was time to prepare to transition to a home of our own.

I shared with our leadership team that it was time to move, and we began to pray for direction. I didn't know where that next place was, but I trusted God to reveal it and provide all we needed. When you are walking in the realm of ridiculous faith, there will be times when it may appear that you don't know what you're doing. The truth is, sometimes you really don't know what you're doing. You're simply trusting God. There are times when you may feel the need to help others understand your decisions and actions when you don't understand them yourself. You're simply obeying God. When you are willing to stay in step with Him, walk in His grace, keeping your eyes on Him, He will lead you to your wealthy place (Psalm 66:12).

> *When you are walking in the realm of ridiculous faith, there will be times when it may appear that you don't know what you're doing. The truth is, sometimes you really don't know what you're doing. You're simply trusting God.*

I've been asked if I ever felt I'd missed God in that move, if I'd thought I'd made a mistake, considering how things played out. I don't. I believe that we were right where the Lord wanted us to be. God always works on multiple levels in multiple ways. Our move was never just about Heirs Covenant Church. It wasn't even about that piece of property. God purposed to transform the hearts of everyone involved, to work through us to advance His Kingdom and impact the City of Hamilton, Ohio. We had an opportunity to do something magnificent in the Kingdom of God—something grander than either congregation could do separately. But God never forces or coerces us into anything. I look back and see that time as a stop on the way to the greater that God had for us, and it was a necessary stop for me and our body. Yes, it had been a test, but those who stayed the course learned and grew stronger in faith because of it. It had prepared us all for the more and had postured us for God's next invitation in the realm of ridiculous faith.

A month later, I was sitting in Pastor Josh Willis's office, talking with him about a piece of property he was selling. God had been speaking to him about a new season in his life. The ending of one season in his life would be the beginning of a new one for me and for Heirs.

As I left that meeting, I knew God had just invited me to level of ridiculous faith like none I'd ever known.

Chapter 16

Stepping into the Promised Land

*"Have I not commanded you? Be strong and of good
courage; do not be afraid, nor be dismayed, for the Lord
your God is with you wherever you go."*
Joshua 1:9

"*Moses, My servant is dead!*" the Lord spoke to Joshua. These words marked a decisive end to one season in the history of Israel. Their time in the wilderness was over, and now it was time to possess the land the Lord had promised them. God was making it clear to Joshua that he needed to abandon any thought of Moses returning to lead them. God, in essence, was telling Joshua, "*What once was is over. Don't look back! It may not look like you thought it would. Now is the time for you to possess what I promised Abraham over 400 years ago. The last 40 years of your life have prepared you for this. Now I AM commissioning you to go forth. I've promised that My Presence will be with you and go before you. It's time to move! Let's go and take the land!*"

We don't read that Joshua hemmed and hawed; we don't read that he bombarded the Lord with a myriad of questions; we don't read that he consulted with the other leaders of Israel to get a consensus. God had spoken. And even though the Lord didn't outline a detailed strategy or plan at that moment, Joshua responded by telling the leaders to tell the people to prepare. "*…Within three days you will cross over this Jordan, to go in to possess the land which the Lord your God is giving you to possess*" (Joshua 1:10,11). Joshua accepted God's invitation into the realm of ridiculous faith.

Joshua could look back over the previous 40 years and recall how the Lord delivered Israel from Egypt. He'd witnessed the parting of the Red Sea. He'd heard the Lord speak at Mount Sinai. He remembered how the Lord kept them, protected them, and provided for them in the wilderness. He'd seen the miracles, the manna, the cloud that led them by day, and the pillar of fire that provided light and warmth at night. Now he had the promise that this same God would be with him as He'd been with Moses. This same God would establish him before the people. This same God would bring him success and lead them into the land.

Be of Good Courage

As we read through the first chapter of Book of Joshua, we see the Lord helping Joshua make a paradigm shift. He had been called and commissioned to lead the Israelites into the land before Moses' death (Deuteronomy 31:23). God is letting Joshua know now is the time to step into his place of leadership. The one thing the Lord emphasized to Joshua over and over was his need to be courageous (Joshua 1: 6,7,9).

Courage is the attitude of facing and dealing with anything perceived as dangerous, difficult, painful, or different rather than withdrawing from it. It is facing challenges with confidence and resolve. The Hebrew word has many meanings, among them: boldness, alertness, determination, firmness. Joshua would need to be bold, firm, and resolute to stand before Israel and speak what God had said. He'd have to display courage to go up against the inhabitants in the land to gain possession of the promise. God had given them the land, but they had to take possession of it.

By the spring of 2018, the Lord had made it clear to me that it was time to move and I would need to step into a new place of leadership—the place He'd been preparing me for all my life. And just like Joshua, I needed to shift paradigms and be courageous. I had to be confident in what the Lord was speaking to me at that moment. I had believed we were where God would plant us to accomplish His plans. Now I had to be courageous enough to stand before our body and speak a word that seemed to contradict what I'd said before. Even though what I'd believed would come to fruition had not happened, God was still speaking to me. He still had an incredible plan for us in the city of

Hamilton, and now we'd be moving again. When He'd spoken to me to "get on the grounds," He was not necessarily speaking of that particular piece of property. He wanted us positioned in the city. He'd established our ministry in Hamilton. He'd connected me with other pastors and leaders in the city. And though I didn't know it then, He was going to further establish our presence in a significant way.

> God knows the way that we take, and each phase of the journey is designed to strengthen us to carry the weight of the greater things He has for us.

There will be times when things just don't go as you anticipated. Let me reemphasize this point: *just because things do not go as anticipated does not mean you missed God!* As you move by faith on a word from the Lord, you will not see the full magnitude of that word. That is why we must continually listen for God's *proceeding* word and remain in lockstep with Holy Spirit.

We must be willing to make whatever adjustments He calls for. He knows the way that we take, and each phase of the journey is designed to strengthen us to carry the weight of the greater things He has for us. We must not allow what *did not* happen to derail us or cause us to lose sight of what God still purposes to do.

The Search Begins

Not long after the Lord said, "You're done," I found out about a building that was for sale.

I was familiar with the building used to host many ministry events, especially for Christian youth. The Underground was located right off I-275, the outer belt of Cincinnati—easily seen from the highway and easily accessed. It seemed like a prime location. I knew the owner, who is a believer, contacted him, and we met. I shared with him our vision for the space that I knew would be named The Embassy.

The owner was asking $700,000. We didn't have that kind of money in the bank, but that didn't faze me. God had proven Himself too many times for me to be hung up on cost. I was prepared to tell our leadership the possibility of moving to The Underground when I received a phone call from one of my pastors. She is a realtor, and she'd come across a property for sale that she thought I needed to see. It was a mile or so away from the building we shared, and it, too, was a building I'd seen before. A former junior high school, 130,000 square feet, sitting on eight acres of land. The price tag—1.7 million.

We made an appointment to see the building; the owner and his realtor met with our realtor and me. We walked through the building—three floors, two gymnasiums, a one-bedroom apartment, ample office space, and classrooms. As I walked through the building, Pastor Josh Willis, the owner, shared with me his original vision for it. When we reached the auditorium, he said, "Here's the crown jewel!" He opened the door to reveal the sanctuary he'd beautifully built out for services. It was an incredible place for worship! Truly a jewel!

We went to Pastor Josh's office, and he asked, "Do you have vision for this place?" I did! I knew this was the place for the Embassy, a place from which we could do all the things God had called us to do. The place that would be an oasis for others. A place from which the Kingdom of God would be seen, demonstrated, and advanced. A place to serve the community, to house faith-based businesses and other ministries. A training place, a healing place, and most importantly, a place for God's Presence to reside and His glory to be reveal in unprecedented ways.

As we left the building, our realtor said, "Congratulations!" I knew she was saying that she believed this was the place God had for us.

I believed it too.

The Choice Is Yours

> *"Will I opt for the one that I know I can easily accomplish, or am I willing to stretch my faith and go for that which can only be achieved by ridiculous faith in God?"*

One of the many things I have learned about living in the realm of ridiculous faith is that as opportunities open for us, we get to choose the level of faith where we are willing to operate. We are presented with options. One is not necessarily better or worse than the other. More likely, one will stretch our faith further than the other. God will say, "You get to choose." As we assess the options before us, we must ask, "Will I opt for the one that I know I can easily accomplish, or am I willing to stretch my faith and go for that which can only be achieved by ridiculous faith in God?"

We were looking at a one-million-dollar difference! I was not daunted by the numbers. The same God who would have to provide $700,000 could just as easily provide 1.7 million. This was not about money, however. God was inviting me—and our entire congregation—to operate in that realm of faith I'd talked about and taught about for years. This would be the most significant step of faith I'd ever made. God was drawing me into this place. He seemed to be saying, "I've given you this message on Ridiculous Faith. Will you put that Word to the test? Will you trust Me like never before? Try Me in this and see what I will do!" The same God who had healed me, the same God who had honored His word in my life so many times, had not changed. I knew what choice I had to make.

> *In that treasure, there's a jewel. This has to do with recovery and restoration of the vision that God has given you.*

Two weeks after seeing the building and talking with Pastor Josh, I drove to Pittsburgh for Covenant Church of Pittsburgh's annual "Presence" conference with Bishop Garlington. The last amen had been said to close the conference, and as I was heading out, I was stopped by Ron Campbell, a powerful man of God from South Africa.

"I have a word for you," he said. I pulled out my phone to record what he had to share. He continued:

> *"So when you were standing out there, the Lord spoke to me and told me there is a treasure to be revealed to you. It's been before you, but you have not had access to it because it's not been the right time. But the time is now. And in that treasure, there's a jewel. This has to do with recovery and restoration of the vision that God has given you."*

As soon as I heard that there was a "jewel" in the treasure, I knew the Lord was letting me know which property was for us.

While that prophetic word had settled things for me, I wanted to give our leadership team opportunity to weigh in. I arranged for them to see The Underground one evening to discuss the possibilities. "Can you see us here?" I asked, and while we knew we'd need to build out sections of the building to adapt to our vision, most felt it was doable, especially in light of our size and finances. But even as we talked that evening, I knew The Underground wasn't the place. It was too small for the vision; the numbers were too easy. It wouldn't require the exercising of great faith, or much faith at all, to secure it. In many ways, I knew we'd be moving backward.

Two weeks later, I took some of those leaders to the school. "Can you see us here?" I asked as we sat in the sanctuary. The responses were mixed. I wasn't at all discouraged by the answers; I'd genuinely wanted and welcomed them. But as I sought God, I saw even more clearly that He had set before me, before us, an opportunity to see the reality of His word come alive in ways we never imagined. He wanted to light a flame in all of us, so we'd know beyond a shadow of doubt that with Him all things really are possible.

It was a defining moment for me, and I would not miss it. By August 2018, I knew I would not settle for anything less than what the Lord had for me. I would extend my faith and believe for something that was far beyond our finances, far beyond our numbers, far beyond our reach. I would trust the God of all possibilities.

You've Not Been This Way Before

Just before Joshua led the children of Israel across the Jordan into the land of promise, we read these words in Joshua 3:1-4:

> ***Then Joshua rose early in the morning; and they set out from Acacia Grove and came to the Jordan, he and all the children of Israel, and lodged there before they crossed over. So it was, after three days, that the officers went through the camp; and they commanded the people, saying, "When you see the ark of the covenant of the Lord your God, and the priests, the Levites, bearing it, then you shall set out from your place and go after it. Yet there shall be a space between you and it, about two thousand cubits by measure. Do not come near it, that you may know the way by which you must go, for you have not passed this way before."***

Joshua and the leaders knew that they were entering into something they'd never known in their history as a nation. Now, rather than having the ark, which represented the presence of God, in the midst of them, it would go before them and lead them. They would need to pace themselves so they could see the way the Lord was taking them. He knew the exact path to take them across the Jordan and into the land they would eventually occupy. Crossing the Jordan was a defining moment for all of Israel.

> *When you and I choose to live in the realm of ridiculous faith, we will face those defining moments. That moment when all you say you believe will be tested. That moment when God asks, "Do you really trust Me like you say you do?"*

When you and I choose to live in the realm of ridiculous faith, we will face those defining moments. That moment when all you say you believe will be tested. That moment when God asks, "Do you *really* trust Me like you say you do?" That moment when you see what is before you—your "Promised Land"— and you know God can do this. You can't be concerned with what others think, say, or do. You are willing to risk it all to see the promise manifest. It's all or nothing! You've reached the point of no return! You must not only be strong and courageous, but you must also position yourself to see God, to hear Him, and move as He moves.

This is the moment God has been preparing you for. Through every circumstance, He has been developing in you the characteristics necessary for living in the realm of ridiculous faith, and you only fully realize it when you accept His invitation and step into that new realm. You have joined the ranks of so many men and women who have dared to stand on God's Word, even when it seemed insane to do so. You have joined the ranks of those who…

- *are not concerned about their reputation*
- *have learned to master the fear of the unknown*
- *are willing to appear foolish in the eyes of men*
- *are willing to take seemingly unreasonable risks*
- *are willing to endure hardship for the sake of the call*

- *are willing to respond in complete obedience to the Lord*
- *are willing to lay down their lives*

Joshua was one of the many individuals we read about in Scripture who exhibited these characteristics. Had these traits not been forged in him, he may never have seen the walls of Jericho fall as they did (Joshua 6). He may have thought it too absurd to pray that the sun stand still until a battle was won (Joshua 10). We may never have read "and he left none remaining" following each conquest.

You may never know your true capacity until you choose to live in this realm of faith. That is when you see what you are capable of by God's grace, favor, and supernatural power operating in your life.

This Is Ridiculous…Faith!

"This is a defining moment for us," I said as I stood before our congregation. I'd called a family meeting to share the opportunity before us, an opportunity that I knew wasn't as much about acquiring a piece of property as it was about walking out the word in real-time. We'd entered into negotiations for the property and had landed at 1.4 million. In the family meeting, we shared our finances openly and honestly as we had always done; it was obvious that the numbers didn't match what was before us. But in the realm of ridiculous faith, that is common. Faith is believing and trusting for that which is beyond your ability, but that which you know is in the heart and mind of the Father for you.

> *You may never know your true capacity until you choose to live in this realm of faith. That is when you see what you are capable of by God's grace, favor, and supernatural power operating in your life.*

At that time, we needed to raise 20%. I asked our body to raise $70,000, and I reached out to some of the ministries and individuals I was in relationship with across the country, asking them to consider sowing into our vision. I fully believed that God would honor our faith. I said to my congregation, "If this doesn't happen, I'm done!" I wanted them to understand how serious I was about this opportunity!

That evening I received two checks, totaling $6,000, one from my wife and one from another dear sister in our body. I believed God was saying, "*I AM pleased. You're headed in the right direction. Keep going!*"

Faith to Forge Ahead

Rarely will you operate in the realm of ridiculous faith without a fight. God had made it clear to Joshua that while He had given the land to Israel, they had to take possession of it! They had to fight! It is the same for you and me. There are obstacles you'll need to overcome. Doors may not immediately open, and you may need to continue to knock until the right one does. God may speak strategies to you that seem a bit, well, ridiculous, and you must be willing to obey.

> *Doors may not immediately open, and you may need to continue to knock until the right one opens. God may speak strategies to you that seem a bit, well, ridiculous, and you must be willing to obey.*

The strategy that God gave Joshua for taking Jericho must have seemed utterly ridiculous to Joshua. Can you imagine the look on the faces of the army when Joshua revealed to them that they would march silently around the city walls for six days and seven times on the seventh day, and then when the priests blew the trumpet, the walls would fall? But God often has unorthodox ways of bringing you and me the victory. We just need to be attentive to His voice and obey His directives. There is never a battle He leads us into that we don't come out the victors when we trust Him.

> *There will be times when you are pursuing the "ridiculous," and the odds are stacked against you... But if you know that God has spoken, you cannot allow the word "no" to deter you.*

It seemed a bit absurd that we'd even consider purchasing property for 1.4 million dollars. But God had spoken, and we had accepted the invitation. We believed He would work it out for us if we didn't give up. Securing financing was a challenge. Pastor Josh, the owner of the property, banked at the same bank, the same branch where we banked, and we both were on a first-name basis with the branch manager. We set up a meeting with her and the mortgage banker to discuss financing, only to be told that we did not have the financial strength. I left the bank disappointed but not defeated. I kept saying, "God's got this worked out. I just need to know how He wants to do it."

There will be times when you are pursuing the "ridiculous," and the odds are stacked against you. Every door seems locked, just like Jericho was locked up. But if you know that God has spoken, you cannot allow the word "no" to deter you. Could it be that God allows the "no's" to see how serious you are about obtaining the promise? Could He be using each "no" to test your resolve?

After that meeting at the bank, I stopped by a store. I was in the parking lot, and the branch manager pulled up next to me.

"John," she said, "I'm so sorry the meeting went the way it did. I didn't expect that. I'm going to give you the name of another bank I believe will do the loan for you. I have a neighbor who banks there. I'll get the name of the bank and the person you should talk with and call you."

She did just that, and I called the bank to set up an appointment. The small commercial bank was a 45-minute drive from me. I met with the vice president, whose family had founded the bank. "You're a man of many talents," he said to me as we sat conversing in his office (he had Googled me). We began discussing the many possibilities. God has a way of setting you in the right situation with the right people—those people you don't have to convince. This was one of those moments, and I knew I was walking in God's favor.

"There are a few ways we can approach it," the VP said.

I walked away from the meeting, knowing the Lord would work through that man and that bank.

Crossing the Finish Line

We now needed to raise the down payment that ended up being 25 percent—$350,000. Throughout November and December, I watched as God graciously and generously brought the resources to us that we needed. Individuals not only in our body but across the country sowed into our vision for The Embassy. One dear friend of mine sowed $50,000!

We'd set December 31, 2018, as our closing date, but we had not raised all the funds needed as that date drew closer. God, however, moved on Pastor Josh's heart. Josh wanted us to have the property. More importantly, he believed that the Lord wanted us to have the property.

"What do you need to raise for the down payment?" he asked.

"We need 25%," I told him.

"I've been praying about it, and I want to help you close this deal. If you come up with $150,000, I will carry the remainder for five years."

Only God could have moved that way! Even with that blessing, as we moved closer to the closing date, we still didn't have all we needed. I was getting concerned that Josh might become anxious that we wouldn't close by the set date. I didn't want to go back to him and say we couldn't close on December 31. I prayed and asked God what we needed to do next. And once again, He moved on our behalf. At Josh's request, because he realized that there were details concerning the property he needed to address, we moved the closing to January. By the second week of January, we had all we needed.

On January 17, 2019, we sat at the table, hearts brimming with gratitude. It was closing day. It was in retrospect that I realized the impeccable timing of God. It had been exactly two years earlier that I stood in the sanctuary of Covenant Church of Pittsburgh and heard Pastor Eric Butler speak these words to me:

There's a present and a ribbon, Apostle John, a golden ribbon that I see being tied in your favor. It's a present that the Lord has wrapped up for you. The Lord says, "Son, I'm going to wrap it up perfectly for you and I'm going to deliver it. It's called a deed. I'm going to continue to work the miracle and the favor of God with the property and the land. I'm going to give you the title deed." Because of all the years that you've been a worshiper and you've led My people in worship… "I've counted all the years; I've counted all the tears. I've captured all the incense and I've taken away all the fears. I've captured this, and I've kept it." says the Lord. "And I'm going to reward you openly and it will be the day of your more," says the Lord.

"Watch the work that I do and perform—even how this thing

begins to turn in your favor, even how grace will be exhibited toward you, even how people will start to come, even how the word will get out that there's a house of worship on the side of the road. I put you there and I will keep you there."

The same God who had spoken those words was the same God who brought them to fruition. He had indeed wrapped it up perfectly and presented it to us—just as He had promised.

I stood on the platform in the sanctuary of The Embassy, the new home of Heirs Covenant Church, looked out over the congregation filled with members and friends who'd come to celebrate the faithfulness and goodness of God with us. As I reflected on the journey that had led to this moment, waves of gratitude swept over me. I had a greater appreciation for the journey—not just my individual journey, but also for the journey of countless others—those whose journeys God miraculously and so seamlessly merged with mine. Those who heard the message and dared to step into the realm of ridiculous with me, those who believed in the vision, heard Holy Spirit and responded in faith, those who stayed the course with me even when it got tough, those who stayed with me when I was still figuring things out, those who prayed for me, those who asked the hard questions and spoke truth in love to me, even those God used to refine me, test me, mature me. Those who trusted the God in me. Together we reaped the blessing that comes from trusting God for what some may deem ridiculous.

As we worshiped together, I was keenly aware that God had just issued yet another invitation to go even deeper into the realm of ridiculous faith.

And we have accepted!

About the Author

John W. Stevenson is founder and CEO of Heirs International Ministries, Heirs Media Group, and Heirs Covenant Church, where he serves as apostle and senior pastor. He is the CEO of The Embassy: A Regional Center for Kindom Transformation, the home of Heirs Covenant Church, Genesis Life and Recovery, and other Kingdom-minded entities.

With over 40 years of ministry experience, John has served as pastor, associate pastor, prophet, teacher, evangelist, worship leader, and chief musician. John is also a songwriter, a music producer, a recording artist, and the author of three books, including *Worshiper by Design: A Unique Look at Why We Were Created*.

Heirs International Ministries' presence is throughout the United States, and Ethiopia, Kenya, South Africa, England, Russia, Barbados, Curacao and Singapore. Through various relationships with Reconciliation! International (Bishop Joseph L. Garlington, also John's pastor), International Worship Institute, the Caribbean Worship Institute, Ambassador Ministries (the late Pastor Moses Vegh), and Oops Asia, a ministry inspiring and impacting Asia through music with a focus on promoting independent artists, the worship influence of H.I.M. has a global impact.

As a music producer, John has recorded 11 projects. John's songs have been recorded by various ministries and artists, including Darwin Hobbs, Bishop Joseph Garlington, David and Nicole Binion, Lenny LeBlanc for Integrity Music, Bishop Paul Morton and Full Gospel Baptist Church. His songs, such as "Arise O God," "You Are Holy", "Under the Shadow," and "Jehovah Reigns," and many others, are sung in churches and at conferences worldwide.

John is co-founder, along with Ford Taylor, of Transformation Cincinnati/Northern Kentucky, a ministry that focuses on city transformation. He served on the Board of Presence Ministries with Glenn Rochelle, Ed Chinn, Howard Rachinski (Founder), and Steve Fry.

He has also served as a Covenant Partner with As One, a group of market place leaders committed to 7 Mountain Initiatives for work place, city and nation transformation. Members of the team included Ford Taylor, Lance Walnau, Os Hillman, to name a few.

John serves in the Business Sphere of The Great Awakening Project, a movement designed to catalyze Awakening in the Church and Revival in America, strategically impacting the 7 Spheres of Influence.

John has led worship for Global Harvest Ministry, a prayer and intercession ministry headed by the late C. Peter Wagner of Fuller Theological Seminary and for The Call, headed by Lou Engle. John has ministered with such individuals as Dr. Bill Hamon of Christian International, the late Dr. Edwin Louis Cole of Christian Men's Network, the late Dr. Myles Munroe, and worship leaders Ron Kenoly, Kent Henry, Marty Nystrom, William Murphy III, and Lamar Boschman. John's ministry and service in the Body of Christ are well respected, diverse and cross racial and denominational lines.

John has a desire and passion to see the Body of Christ mature and walk in Kingdom influence, Kingdom impact with Kingdom results. John is married to the lovely Marissa Stevenson, and they are the parents of four sons, one daughter, three daughters-in-love and the grandparents of ten grandchildren.

Also by John W. Stevenson
Nothing But the Truth: A Lifestyle of Christian Integrity
The Second Flood: The Discipine of Worship
Worshiper by Design: A Unique Look at Why We Were Created

To learn more about the ministry of John W. Stevenson, visit: www.jwstevenson.com

www.ingramcontent.com/pod-product-compliance
Lightning Source LLC
Chambersburg PA
CBHW071930290426
44110CB00013B/1545